INTENSE ILLUSTRATIONS

A NEW COLLECTION OF ILLUSTRATIONS, STORIES AND QUOTES TO GET YOUR MESSAGES GOING

JIM BURNS AND MIKE DeVRIES

Gospel Light

Gospel Light is an evangelical Christian publisher dedicated to serving the local church. We believe God's vision for Gospel Light is to provide church leaders with biblical, user-friendly materials that will help them evangelize, disciple and minister to children, youth and families.

It is our prayer that this Gospel Light resource will help you discover biblical truth for your own life and help you minister to youth. May God richly bless you.

For a free catalog of resources from Gospel Light, please contact your Christian supplier or contact us at 1-800-4-GOSPEL *or* www.gospellight.com.

PUBLISHING STAFF
William T. Greig, Chairman
Kyle Duncan, Publisher
Dr. Elmer L. Towns, Senior Consulting Publisher
Pam Weston, Senior Editor
Patti Pennington Virtue, Associate Editor
Jeff Kempton, Editorial Assistant
Hilary Young, Editorial Assistant
Bayard Taylor, M.Div., Senior Editor, Biblical and Theological Issues
Kevin Parks, Cover Designer
Roseanne Richardson, Cover Production
Debi Thayer, Designer

ISBN 0-8307-2920-8
© 2002 Gospel Light
All rights reserved.
Printed in the U.S.A.

HOW TO MAKE CLEAN COPIES
FROM THIS BOOK

Dedication

To Bob Campbell

Thank you for the many years of being a champion for the YouthBuilders' cause and a mentor to me. Your words and life have challenged us to stretch beyond our comfort zone to make a greater impact. Thank you, Bob, for your enthusiasm and wisdom. Your fingerprints are all over our ministry.

—Mike DeVries

Contents

Acknowledgments 8
Introduction 9

Illustrations and Stories

Abraham Lincoln 12
    Even one of our greatest presidents failed many times in his life.
All It Takes Is a Little Motivation .14
    Motivation is the difference between giving up or pushing forward.
Are You God? 16
    Our actions can provide others with a picture of God.
A Beautiful Web 18
    Looks can be deceiving.
Bobby and the Special Gift 20
    We should bless others as God has blessed us.
Butch O'Hare 23
    Great things can happen when we turn our lives over to God.
College Professor in Fiji 25
    The Word of God has the power to transform us in miraculous ways.
The Cracked Pot 27
    What we see as flaws can be wonderful tools for God.
The Damage of Gossip 29
    Gossip spreads easily, but its damage isn't easily repaired.
The Definition of Success 31
    The measure of success is in the state of your heart.
Discouraged? 32
    Don't focus on the details to the point of losing the vision of the end result.
The Doll and the White Rose 33
    There is nothing more powerful than love.
Emperor Ling 36
    Honesty is more valuable than appearances.
Facing Obstacles 39
    God often uses challenges to strengthen our faith.
Fish Feeding 41
    We need God's Word in our daily lives to be spiritually healthy.
The Football Game 42
    Our heavenly Father is our biggest fan.
Forgiveness 45
    God forgives even the lowliest of His children.
Frederick the Great, King of Prussia 47
    Do not be afraid to confess your sins to God.
Getting Knocked Down 49
    Everyone fails sometimes; those who succeed are the ones who keep trying.
Giving and Receiving—A Circle of Love 50
    God abundantly repays us when we share His blessings with others.
Giving to Others 51
    There is joy and blessing in filling the needs of others by sharing what we have.
God's Children Are Heirs 53
    Through Christ we inherit God's blessings.
God's Strength Through Our Weakness 55
    In our weakness we can recognize the strength of God.

High-Dive Conversion 57
 Jesus' sacrifice on the cross showed God's desire to reconcile us to Himself.
How Do You Live Your Dash? 59
 How we live our lives matters to God.
Letter from a Friend 61
 God reveals Himself every day; do we see Him?
Letter from Sister Mary Rose 63
 "I love you" is a powerful phrase.
Eric Liddell 66
 Sometimes the greatest stories are the ones untold.
The Little Boy Who Wanted to Fight Fires 69
 Don't let doubt or fear keep you from following your heart.
Littleton's Martyrs 71
 We are called to remain steadfast in our faith; our reward awaits us in heaven.
Lost in the Desert 74
 Trusting in what we cannot see can bring about great surprises.
Mathilde 76
 Keeping up appearances can be too costly.
Momentary Pleasures, Lasting Pain 78
 Our sin affects more than just us.
The Most Caring Child 80
 A child's point of view can be profound.
No Favoritism Allowed 81
 Each one of us, regardless of appearance or position, deserves love and respect.
Observation Is the Key 82
 Test everything against the Word of God.
The Poison Tongue 84
 Words may be temporary, but their impact can last a lifetime.
The Power of Encouragement 86
 Kind words go a long way.
The Power of Hope 90
 Hope gives us the incentive to keep striving toward our goals.
The Power of Prayer 92
 Prayer knows no boundaries.
Pushing Against the Rock 94
 Following God's will strengthens us.
Remembering to Forget 96
 Holding a grudge only hurts the person carrying it.
The Royal Robe 97
 To be transformed by God we must be willing to give up everything.
Say a Prayer 100
 Sometimes prayer is exactly what is needed.
Spend Time Wisely 101
 Each day is a gift from God.
Standing Firm in Faith 103
 The depth of our faith is often revealed in difficult situations.
Staying Connected 105
 Fellowship and community are vital.
Telemachus 106
 Standing up for your faith can have an impact you cannot imagine.
The Test 109
 True beauty is seen from the heart.

Those with the Least Sometimes Give the Most 112
 Having true wealth means being rich in faith.
True Beauty 116
 Outer beauty fades—inner beauty is what's important.
The True Meaning of the Candy Cane 118
 There is more to a candy cane than peppermint flavor!
Trust and Obey 120
 Trusting God means obeying His commands without questioning why.
Two Nickels and Five Pennies 121
 Look for the good in every situation.
The Value of Knowing Jesus 122
 A relationship with Jesus brings eternal life.
What If 125
 What if we loved God with the same passion with which He loves us?

Funnies

Albert Einstein and His Chauffeur 128
And You Thought You Had Problems 129
Are You an Optimist or a Pessimist? 130
Carjacking Foiled 131
A Church Split 132
Didn't Want to Go to Church 132
Dinner Guests 133
The Elevator 133
Freefall 134
God Will Provide 135
God's Creation 136
Only Opportunities 136
Payback 137
School Excuses 138
Through the Eyes of a Child 139
Two Monks 139
Value This Time in Your Life 140
Van Gogh's Family 141

Quotes

Attitude 143
Character 147
Children and Family 148
Evangelism 149
God 151
Kindness 152
Love 153
Funny but True 155

Contributors
Contributors 156

Indexes

Scripture 157
Topical 161

Acknowledgments

A very special thanks to Carrie Hicks Steele. I handed you my favorite illustrations, quotes and funnies and you turned it into a book. Your loyalty, work ethic, integrity, purity and drive for excellence are a daily inspiration.

Thank you to my own daughter, Rebecca Burns, for the great work you did on this project. I loved having you in our office for your summer job. I'm so very proud of you.

Thank you to the many YouthBuilders associates who sent in their favorite stories and quotes to me. You are amazing people doing a most extraordinary work with kids and families. A very special thanks to Jean Tippit, Jim Liebelt, Eric Wakeling and John Murphy for the more than excellent job you did on taking the stories and turning them into helpful tools with the addition of the application and Scripture. You are all such special friends and oh so talented.

—Jim Burns

Life is an illustration and a quote. My life is a constant quest for the right illustration and quote. I have found them in books and on billboards, and I actually found one recently on a bathroom wall! (It was clean!) If you are holding this book, then you are no doubt on the same quest for life-changing illustrations. These illustrations, quotes and funnies are ones I have been using for the last few years.

At YouthBuilders, we ask our 500 plus associates to send us their best stuff. We search the Internet. We borrow from great speakers. Some of the material comes simply from life experiences and others took years to craft just right. We don't remember where we got some of these incredible stories and quotes. We do know they have worked for us.

I like to look at illustrations, quotes and even funny stories as paintings. The point of a message is sometimes unclear until you provide just the right illustration for it. Jesus, the master storyteller, is our hero and leader in painting the incredible story just right to make the point come alive. He took everyday, ordinary life experiences and taught the words of eternal truth.

There is nothing quite like sitting at the feet of a great communicator. What we have tried to do with this volume is to take some of the best material from some of the finest communicators and offer them directly to you. We know these illustrations can make a difference in your life and the lives of those to whom you speak because they already have done so in our own lives.

Blessings,
Jim Burns, Ph.D.
President, YouthBuilders

Introduction

Illustrations and Stories

Abraham Lincoln

KEY VERSE

Jesus replied, "No one who puts his hand to the plow and looks back is fit for service in the kingdom of God."
Luke 9:62

APPLICATION

Never give up or turn back. God is not keeping score; He just wants you to finish the race.

ADDITIONAL SCRIPTURES

Philippians 1:6; 4:13; 2 Timothy 4:7

ILLUSTRATION

Abraham Lincoln was born into poverty and faced defeat throughout his whole life. He lost eight elections, twice failed in business and suffered a nervous breakdown. He could have quit many times—but he didn't, and because he didn't quit, he became one of the greatest presidents in the history of our country.

1816—At the age of seven he went to work to help support his family after losing their home.
1818—His mother died.
1831—He failed in business.
1832—He ran for the state legislature and lost. He lost his job. He wanted to go to law school but couldn't get in.

1833—He borrowed some money from a friend to begin a business. By the end of the year he was bankrupt, and he spent the next 17 years of his life paying off this debt.

1834—He ran for the state legislature again and won.

1835—He was engaged to be married, but his heart was broken when his sweetheart died.

1836—He had a total nervous breakdown and was in bed for six months.

1838—He sought to become speaker of the state legislature and lost.

1840—He sought to become an elector and lost.

1843—He ran for Congress and lost.

1846—He ran for Congress again—this time he won, went to Washington and did a good job.

1848—He ran for reelection to Congress and lost.

1849—He sought the job of land officer in his home state and lost.

1854—He ran for the Senate of the United States and lost.

1856—He sought the nomination for vice president at his party's national convention and received fewer than 100 votes.

1858—He ran for the United States Senate again—and lost again.

1860—He was elected president of the United States.

The path was worn and slippery. My foot slipped from under me, knocking the other out of the way, but I recovered and said to myself, "It's a slip and not a fall."

—Abraham Lincoln

All It Takes Is a Little Motivation

KEY VERSE

But seek first his kingdom and his righteousness, and all these things will be given to you as well.
Matthew 6:33

APPLICATION

What motivates you? What drives you? What makes you tick? It should be the love and power of God Himself.

ADDITIONAL SCRIPTURES

Matthew 6:1-4; John 12:42-46; Galatians 1:10; 1 John 5:2-13

ILLUSTRATION

A gentleman worked the 4:00 P.M.-to-midnight shift. He always walked home after work. One night the moon was shining so brightly, he decided to take a shortcut through the cemetery, which would save him roughly a half-mile walk.

Nothing happened, so he repeated the process on a regular basis, always following the same path.

One night as he was walking his route through the cemetery, he did not realize that during the day a grave had been dug in the very center of his regular path. He stepped right into the grave and immediately started desperately trying to get out. His best efforts failed him, and after a few minutes, he decided to relax and wait until morning when someone would help him out.

He sat down in the corner and was half asleep when a drunk stumbled into the grave. His arrival roused the shift

worker since the drunk was desperately trying to climb out, clawing frantically at the sides. Our hero reached out his hand, touched the drunk on the leg and said, "Friend, you can't get out of here."

Suddenly, the drunk jumped so high that he was able to climb right out of the grave. Now *that's* motivation!

Contributed by
Jean Tippit

Are You God?

KEY VERSE

Dear children, let us not love with words or tongue but with actions and in truth.
1 John 3:18

APPLICATION

The world will recognize you as a child of God when you show the love of God through your actions.

ADDITIONAL SCRIPTURES

Deuteronomy 15:7-11; Matthew 25:31-46; John 14:23-24; 1 John 3:16-17,19-23

ILLUSTRATION

Shortly after World War II came to a close, Europeans began picking up the pieces. Much of the Old Country had been ravaged by the war and was in ruins. Perhaps the saddest sight of all was that of little orphaned children starving in the streets of those war-torn cities.

Early one chilly morning, an American soldier was making his way back to the barracks in London. As he passed a doughnut shop, he saw a little boy staring into the window. The soldier turned the corner in his Jeep, got out and walked quietly over to the where the little fellow was standing. Through the steamed-up window he could see the mouth-watering morsels as they were being pulled from the oven, piping hot. The boy salivated and released a slight groan as he watched the cook place them into the glass-enclosed counter ever so carefully.

The soldier's heart went out to the nameless orphan

standing beside him. "Son, would you like some of those?" the soldier asked.

The boy was startled. "Oh yes, I would!" he exclaimed.

The soldier stepped inside and bought a dozen of the freshest doughnuts, put them in a bag and walked back to where the lad was standing in the foggy cold of the London morning. He smiled, held out the warm bag and said simply, "Here you are, young man."

As he turned to walk away, the soldier felt a tug on his coat. He turned around and the child asked quietly, "Mister, are you God?"

We are never more like God than when we give (see John 3:16).

A Beautiful Web

KEY VERSE

Enter through the narrow gate. For wide is the gate and broad is the road that leads to destruction, and many enter through it. But small is the gate and narrow the road that l eads to life, and only a few find it.
Matthew 7:13-14

APPLICATION

The fact that everybody is doing it does not make it right—or even safe!

ADDITIONAL SCRIPTURES

Psalm 41:10; Luke 13:22-38; Romans 6:23; 12:1-2; 1 John 2:15-17

ILLUSTRATION

Once upon a time, Old Man Spider built a beautiful web in an old house. He kept it clean and shiny so that flies would patronize it. The minute he got a customer, he would make a quick meal of it and was very careful to clean up afterward so that other flies would not get suspicious.

One day Fairly Intelligent Fly came buzzing by the clean spiderweb. Old Man Spider called out, "Come in and sit."

But Fairly Intelligent Fly replied, "No, sir. I don't see other flies in your house, and I am not going in alone!"

Right about then Fairly Intelligent Fly noticed a large

crowd of flies dancing around on a piece of brown paper below. He was delighted and prepared to join the crowd. Just before he landed, Big Bee zoomed by, calling out, "Don't land there, stupid! That's flypaper!"

But Fairly Intelligent Fly shouted back, "Don't be silly. Those flies are dancing down there! Everybody's doing it. That many flies can't be wrong!" And he landed—permanently.

Some of us want to be with the crowd so badly that we end up in a mess. What does it profit to escape the web only to end up stuck in the glue?

Bobby and the Special Gift

KEY VERSE

Freely you have received, freely give.
Matthew 10:8

APPLICATION

The proper response to what Jesus has done for us is for us to love and serve others.

ADDITIONAL SCRIPTURES

John 13:14-15,34; 15:12; Galatians 5:13; Ephesians 6:7

ILLUSTRATION

Bobby was getting cold sitting out in his backyard in the snow. Bobby didn't wear boots because he didn't like them and besides that, he didn't own any. The thin sneakers he wore had a few holes in them and they did a poor job of keeping out the cold.

Bobby had been in his backyard for about an hour already. And try as he might, he could not come up with an idea for his mother's Christmas gift. He shook his head as he thought, *This is useless; even if I do come up with an idea, I don't have any money to spend.* Ever since his father had died three years ago, the family of five had struggled. It wasn't because his mother didn't care or try; there just never seemed to be enough. She worked nights at the hospital, but the small wage she earned could only be stretched so far.

What the family lacked in money and material things,

they more than made up for in love and family unity.
Bobby had three sisters, two older and one younger.
Together, the four children ran the household in their
mother's absence. All three of Bobby's sisters had already
made beautiful gifts for their mother. Somehow it just
wasn't fair. Here it was Christmas Eve already, and Bobby
had nothing to give his mother. Wiping a tear from his
eye, Bobby kicked the snow and started to walk down to
the street where the shops and stores were. It wasn't easy
being six years old and without a father, especially when
he needed a man to talk to.

Bobby wandered from shop to shop, looking into each
decorated window. Everything seemed so beautiful and
so out of reach. It was starting to get dark, so Bobby
reluctantly turned to walk back home when suddenly his
eyes caught the glimmer of the setting sun's rays reflect-
ing off of something along the curb. He reached down
and discovered a shiny dime. Never before had anyone
felt so wealthy as Bobby felt at that moment. As he held
his newfound treasure, a warmth spread throughout his
entire body and he walked into the first store he saw. His
excitement quickly turned cold when salesperson after
salesperson told him that he could not buy anything with
only a dime.

Then Bobby saw a flower shop and went inside to wait
in line with the other last-minute shoppers. When it was
finally his turn, Bobby presented the dime and asked if he
could buy one flower for his mother's Christmas gift. The
shopkeeper looked at Bobby and his 10-cent offering.
Then he put his hand on Bobby's shoulder and said to
him, "You just wait here and I'll see what I can do for you."

As Bobby waited, he looked at the beautiful flowers.
Even though he was a boy, he could see why mothers and
girls liked flowers. The sound of the door closing as the
last customer left jolted Bobby back to reality. All alone in
the shop, Bobby began to feel alone and afraid.

Suddenly the shopkeeper came out from the back of
the store and walked over to the counter. There, before
Bobby's eyes, lay twelve long stemmed red roses, with
leaves of green and tiny white flowers all tied together
with a big silver bow. Bobby's heart sank as the owner
picked them up and placed them gently into a long white
box.

"That will be 10 cents, young man," the shopkeeper
said reaching out his hand for the dime. Slowly, Bobby
moved his hand to give the man his dime. Could this be

true? No one else would give him a thing for his dime! Sensing the boy's reluctance, the shopkeeper added, "I just happened to have some roses on sale for 10 cents a dozen. Would you like them?"

This time Bobby did not hesitate, and when the man placed the long box into his hands, he knew it was true. Walking out the door that the owner was holding open for Bobby, he heard the shopkeeper say, "Merry Christmas, son." As he returned inside, the shopkeeper's wife walked out and asked him, "Who were you talking to back there and where are the roses you were fixing?"

Staring out the window, the shopkeeper blinked back the tears forming in his eyes and replied, "A strange thing happened to me this morning. While I was setting up things to open the shop, I thought I heard a voice telling me to set aside a dozen of my best roses for a special gift. I wasn't sure at the time whether I had lost my mind, but I set them aside anyway. Then just a few minutes ago, a little boy came into the shop and wanted to buy a flower for his mother with one small dime. When I looked at him, I saw myself many years ago. I too was a poor boy with nothing to buy my mother a Christmas gift. A bearded man, whom I never knew, stopped me on the street and told me that he wanted to give me 10 dollars. When I saw that little boy tonight, I knew to whom that voice belonged, and I put together a dozen of my very best roses."

The shopkeeper and his wife hugged each other tightly, and as they stepped out into the bitter cold air, somehow they didn't feel cold at all.

Butch O'Hare

KEY VERSE

*If anyone is in Christ, he is a new creation;
the old has gone, the new has come!*
2 Corinthians 5:17

APPLICATION

It's never too late to start a new life in Christ.

ADDITIONAL SCRIPTURES

John 3:16-21; Galatians 6:15; Ephesians 4:22-24; Titus 3:3-8

ILLUSTRATION

During World War II, many people gained fame in one way or another. One man was Butch O'Hare, a fighter pilot assigned to an aircraft carrier in the Pacific. One time his squadron was assigned to fly a particular mission. After he was airborne, Butch looked at his fuel gauge and realized that someone had forgotten to top off his fuel tank. Because of this, he would not have enough fuel to complete his mission and get back to his ship. His flight leader told him to leave formation and return.

As he was returning to the mother ship, he could see a squadron of Japanese Zeroes heading toward the fleet to attack. With all the fighter planes gone, the fleet was almost defenseless. He was the only opportunity to distract and divert them.

Single-handedly, he dove into the formation of Japanese planes and attacked them. Butch dove at the would-be attackers and fought until all his ammunition was gone; then he dove and tried to clip off a wing or tail

or anything that would make the enemy planes unfit to fly. He did anything he could to keep them from reaching the American ships.

Finally, the Japanese squadron took off in another direction; and Butch O'Hare and his fighter, both badly shot, limped back to the carrier. The American fighter planes were rigged with cameras so that as they flew and fought, pictures were taken, so pilots could learn more about the terrain, enemy maneuvers, etc.; and although Butch told his story, it was not until the film from his plane's camera was developed that the extent to which he went to protect his fleet was realized. He was recognized as a hero and given one of the nation's highest military honors and had an airport named after him—maybe you've heard of it.

There was also a man named Easy Eddie, a Chicago lawyer who worked for the notorious Al Capone, a seedy and dangerous criminal. Easy Eddie was a very good lawyer; in fact, because of his skill, he was able to keep Al Capone out of jail many times.

To show his appreciation, Al Capone paid Easy Eddie very well and gave him many things, including a home with a fenced-in property that filled an entire Chicago city block. Easy Eddie had live-in help and all the conveniences of the day.

Easy Eddie also had a son. He loved his son immensely and gave him all the best things—clothes, cars and a good education. Because he loved his son so much, Easy Eddie tried to teach him right from wrong, but the one thing he couldn't give his son was a good name and a good example.

Easy Eddie decided that his son needed these things more than all the riches could buy, so he went to the authorities in order to rectify the wrongs he had done. Telling the truth to the authorities meant testifying against Al Capone.

Easy Eddie knew that Al Capone would do his best to have him killed because of his testimony, but he wanted more than anything to be an example for his son—to do the best he could to give back to his son a good name. So he testified and within a year, Easy Eddie was shot and killed on a lonely street in Chicago.

These might sound like two unrelated stories, but Easy Eddie's son did grow up to be quite a man of honor and integrity, who made his family name proud. Who was he? Butch O'Hare, of course!

Contributed by
Jill Corey

College Professor in Fiji

KEY VERSE

All Scripture is God-breathed and is useful for teaching, rebuking, correcting and training in righteousness, so that the man of God may be thoroughly equipped for every good work.
2 Timothy 3:16-17

APPLICATION

The Word of God can be transforming and life changing. Read it carefully.

ADDITIONAL SCRIPTURES

Psalm 119:11,105; John 8:31-36; 15:7-14; Hebrews 4:11-13; 1 John 2:7-17

ILLUSTRATION

The story is told of a college professor who visited the islands of Fiji. An agnostic, he critically remarked to an elderly chief, "You're a great leader, but it's a pity you've been taken in by those foreign missionaries. They only want to get rich through you. No one believes the Bible anymore. People are tired of the threadbare story of Christ dying on a cross for the sins of mankind. They know better now. I'm sorry you've been so foolish as to accept their story."

The old chief's eyes flashed as he answered, "Do you see that great rock over there? On it we used to smash the heads of our victims. And there," he said, pointing, "notice the furnace next to the rock? It was in that oven that we formerly roasted the bodies of our enemies

before we ate them. If it hadn't been for those good missionaries and the love of Jesus that changed us from cannibals into Christians, you'd never leave this place alive! You'd better thank the Lord for the gospel; otherwise, we'd already be feasting on you. If it weren't for the Bible, we'd be having you for supper!"

The Cracked Pot

KEY VERSE

*My grace is sufficient for you, for my power
is made perfect in weakness.*
2 Corinthians 12:9

APPLICATION

In our weakness, God works in ways that we may not
comprehend. When we are weak, we rely on God's Spirit
to do the work to fulfill His plan, not ours.

**ADDITIONAL
SCRIPTURES**

Exodus 15:2; 1 Corinthians 1:27; Hebrews 11:32-34

ILLUSTRATION

A water bearer had two large pots, each hung on an end
of a pole, which he carried across his neck. One of the
pots had a crack in it, and while the other pot was perfect
and always delivered a full portion of water at the end of
the long walk from the stream to the master's house, the
cracked pot arrived only half full. For two years this went
on daily, with the bearer delivering only one and a half
pots of water to his master's house. Of course, the perfect
pot was proud of its accomplishments, perfect to the end
for which it was made.

But the poor cracked pot was ashamed of its own
imperfection and miserable that it was able to accomplish
only half of what it had been made to do.

After two years of what it perceived to be a bitter failure, it spoke to the water bearer one day by the stream.
"I am ashamed of myself, and I want to apologize to
you."

"Why?" asked the bearer. "What are you ashamed of?"

"I have been able, for these past two years, to deliver only half my load because this crack in my side causes water to leak out all the way back to your master's house. Because of my flaws, you have to do all of this work, and you don't get full value from your efforts," the pot said.

The water bearer felt sorry for the old cracked pot, and in his compassion he said, "As we return to the master's house, I want you to notice the beautiful flowers along the path."

Indeed, as they went up the hill, the old cracked pot took notice of the sun warming the beautiful wild flowers on the side of the path, and this cheered it some. But at the end of the trail, it still felt badly because it had leaked out half its load, and so again it apologized to the bearer for its failure.

The bearer said to the pot, "Did you notice that there were flowers only on your side of the path but not on the other pot's side? That's because I have always known about your flaw, and I took advantage of it. I planted flower seeds on your side of the path, and every day while we walk back from the stream, you've watered them. For two years I have been able to pick these beautiful flowers to decorate my master's table. Without you being just the way you are, he would not have this beauty to grace his house."

Each of us has our own unique flaws. We're all cracked pots. But if we will allow Him, the Lord will use our flaws to grace His table. In God's great economy, nothing goes to waste.

The Damage of Gossip

KEY VERSE

*A perverse man stirs up dissension, and
a gossip separates close friends.*
Proverbs 16:28

APPLICATION

Nothing is more deadly to relationships than spreading false rumors and gossip. The wise person will keep his or her tongue in check.

ADDITIONAL SCRIPTURES

Leviticus 19:16; Psalm 15:2-4; Proverbs 10:19; 11:13; 15:4; 18:21; Matthew 12:35-37; 1 Timothy 5:13; James 3:1-12

ILLUSTRATION

A woman repeated a bit of gossip about a neighbor. Within a few days the whole community knew the story. The person who was the obnject of the gossip was deeply hurt and offended. Later, the woman responsible for spreading the rumor learned that it was completely untrue. She was very sorry and went to a wise old sage to find out what she could do to repair the damage.

"Go to the marketplace," he said, "and purchase a chicken and have it killed. Then on your way home, pluck its feathers and drop them one by one along the road. Then come back tomorrow and I will tell you what else to do." Although she was surprised by this advice, the woman did what she was told.

The next day, the woman visited the wise man again. He said, "Now go and collect all those feathers you dropped yesterday and bring them back to me."

The woman followed the same road she had the day before, but to her dismay the wind had blown all the feathers away. After searching for hours, she returned to the wise man with only three feathers in her hand.

"You see," said the old sage, "it's easy to drop them, but it's impossible to get them back. So it is with gossip; it doesn't take much to spread a rumor, but once you do, you can never completely undo the damage."

The Definition of Success

KEY VERSE

Do you not know that in a race all the runners run, but only one gets the prize? Run in such a way as to get the prize. Everyone who competes in the games goes into strict training. They do it to get a crown that will not last; but we do it to get a crown that will last forever.
1 Corinthians 9:24-25

 **APPLICATION**

Success is not measured by the amount of things you have at the end of life but the joy of serving the Lord and the rewards of living for Him.

 **ADDITIONAL SCRIPTURES**

Proverbs 2; 3:5-6; Ecclesiastes 12:13-14; Romans 12:9-19; Philippians 3:12-16; Hebrews 12:1-2

ILLUSTRATION

To laugh often and much;

To win the respect of intelligent people and the affection of children;

To earn the appreciation of honest critics and endure the betrayal of false friends;

To appreciate beauty;

To find the best in others;

To leave the world a bit better, whether by a healthy child, a redeemed social condition or a job well done;

To know even one life has breathed easier because you have lived—this is to have succeeded.

Discouraged?

KEY VERSE

We are hard pressed on every side, but not crushed; perplexed, but not in despair; persecuted, but not abandoned; struck down, but not destroyed.
2 Corinthians 4:8-9

APPLICATION

Always look to the end of something and not at the points along the way; the bad ones can discourage us and the good ones can keep us celebrating a little too long.

ADDITIONAL SCRIPTURES

Psalm 37:23-24; 2 Timothy 2:10-13; 1 John 5:4-5

ILLUSTRATION

As I was driving home from work one day, I stopped to watch a local little league baseball game being played in a park near my home. As I sat down behind the bench on the first-base line, I asked one of the boys what the score was.

"We're behind 14 to nothing," he answered with a smile.

"Really," I said. "I have to say you don't look very discouraged."

"Why should we be discouraged?" the boy asked with a puzzled look on his face. "We haven't been up to bat yet."

The Doll and the White Rose

KEY VERSE

For the wages of sin is death,
but the gift of God is eternal life in
Christ Jesus our Lord.
Romans 6:23

APPLICATION

When we abuse drugs or alcohol we not only hurt ourselves but also risk destroying the lives of others.

ALTERNATIVE APPLICATION

The childlike faith of the little boy was strong enough and innocent enough to allow God to work a miracle in his life.

ADDITIONAL SCRIPTURES

Isaiah 5:22; Matthew 18:3-4; Luke 17:5-6; Romans 13:13-14; 1 Peter 4:3-5

ILLUSTRATION

I hurried into the local department store to grab some last-minute Christmas gifts. I looked at all the people and grumbled to myself. I would be in here forever and I had so much to do. Christmas was beginning to become such a drag. I kind of wished that I could just sleep through Christmas. But I hurried as best I could through all the

people to the toy department. Once again I kind of mumbled to myself at the prices of all these toys and wondered if the grandkids would even play with them.

As I wandered into the doll aisle, I noticed a little boy about five years old holding a lovely doll. He kept touching her hair and he held her so gently. I could not seem to help myself. I just kept looking over at the little boy and wondered who the doll was for. I watched him as he turned to a woman he called Auntie and said, "Are you sure I don't have enough money?"

She replied, a bit impatiently, "Yes, I'm sure—you do not have enough money for that doll."

Then the aunt told the little boy not to go anywhere and that she had to go get some other things and would be back in a few minutes.

The boy continued to hold the doll after his aunt left the aisle. After a bit, I asked him who the doll was for. He replied, "It's the doll my sister wanted so badly for Christmas. She just knew that Santa would bring it."

I told him that there was still time for Santa to bring it. He said, "No, Santa can't go where my sister is. I have to give the doll to my mama to take to her."

I asked him where his sister was. He looked at me with the saddest eyes and said, "She went to be with Jesus. My daddy says that Mama is going to have to go be with her."

My heart nearly stopped beating. Then the boy looked at me again and said, "I told my daddy to tell Mama not to go yet. I told him to tell her to wait 'til I got back from the store."

Then he asked me if I wanted to see his picture. I told him I would love to. He pulled out some pictures he'd had taken at the front of the store. He said, "I want my mama to take this with her, so she won't ever forget me. I love my mama so very much and I wish she didn't have to leave me. But Daddy says she needs to be with my sister."

I saw that the little boy had lowered his head and had grown very quiet.

While he was not looking, I reached into my purse and pulled out a handful of bills. I asked the little boy, "Shall we count that money one more time?"

He grew excited and said "Yes, I just know it has to be enough." So I slipped my money in with his and we began to count it. Of course it was plenty for the doll. He softly said, "Thank You, Jesus, for giving me enough money." Then he looked at me and said, "I only asked

Jesus to give me enough money to buy this doll, so Mama can take it with her to give to my sister. And He heard my prayer. I wanted to ask Him for enough to buy my mama a white rose, but I didn't. Even so, He gave me enough for that too! My mama loves white roses so very, very much."

In a few minutes the aunt came back and I wheeled my cart away. I could not keep from thinking about the little boy as I finished my shopping in a totally different spirit than when I had started.

And I kept remembering a story I had seen in the newspaper several days earlier about a drunk driver hitting a car and killing a little girl and that the mother was in serious condition. The family was deciding about whether or not to remove her from the life-support system. Now surely this little boy did not belong with that story.

Two days later I read in the paper that the family had disconnected the life support and the young woman had died. I could not forget the little boy and just kept wondering if the two were somehow connected. Later that same day, I could not help myself—I went out and bought some white roses and took them to the funeral home where the young woman was. And there she was holding a lovely white rose, the beautiful doll and the picture of the little boy in the store. I left there in tears, my life changed forever. The love that little boy had for his little sister and his mother was overwhelming. And in a split second a drunk driver had ripped the life of that little boy to pieces.

Contributed by
Craig Coon

Emperor Ling

KEY VERSE

The LORD detests lying lips, but he delights in men who are truthful.
Proverbs 12:22

APPLICATION

Just like this emperor sought the honest person, so the Lord seeks honest people to be used by Him. The Lord rewards those who are truthful.

ADDITIONAL SCRIPTURES

Psalm 15; Proverbs 12:17; 16:13; 2 Corinthians 6:3-7

ILLUSTRATION

Once there was an emperor in the Far East who was growing old and knew it was time to choose his successor. Instead of choosing one of his assistants or one of his own children, he decided to do something different. He called all the young people in the kingdom together one day. He said, "It has come time for me to step down and to choose the next emperor. I have decided to choose one of you."

The children were shocked! But the emperor continued, "I am going to give each one of you a seed today. One seed. It is a very special seed. I want to you to go home, plant the seed, water it and come back here one year from today with what you have grown from this one seed. I will then judge the plants that you bring to me, and the one who grew the plant I choose will be the next emperor of the kingdom!"

There was one boy named Ling who was there that day and he, like the others, received a seed. He went home and excitedly told his mother the whole story. She helped him get a pot and some planting soil, and he planted the seed and watered it carefully. Every day he would water it and watch to see if it had grown. After about three weeks, the other youths began to talk about their seeds and plants that were beginning to grow.

Ling kept going home and checking his seed, but nothing ever grew. Three weeks, four weeks, five weeks went by. Still nothing. By now all the others were talking about their plants, but Ling didn't have a plant and he felt like a failure. Six months went by—still nothing in Ling's pot. He just knew he had killed his seed. Everyone else had trees and tall plants, but he had nothing. Ling didn't say anything to his friends, however. He just kept waiting for his seed to grow.

A year finally went by and all the youths of the kingdom brought their plants to the emperor for inspection. Ling told his mother that he wasn't going to take an empty pot. But she encouraged him to go and to take his pot and to be honest about what happened. Ling felt sick to his stomach, but he knew his mother was right. He took his empty pot to the palace.

When Ling arrived, he was amazed by all the different plants grown by all the other youths. They were beautiful and in all shapes and sizes. Ling put his empty pot on the floor and many of the other kids laughed at him. A few felt sorry for him and just said, "Hey, nice try."

When the emperor arrived, he surveyed the room and greeted the young people. Ling tried to hide in the back of the room. "My, what great plants, trees and flowers you have grown," said the emperor. "Today one of you will be appointed the next emperor."

Suddenly, the emperor spotted Ling in the back of the room with his empty pot. He ordered his guards to bring him to the front. Ling was terrified. *The emperor knows I'm a failure! Maybe he will have me killed!* he thought.

When Ling got to the front, the emperor asked his name. "My name is Ling," he replied. All of others in the room laughed and made fun of him. The emperor commanded everyone to be silent. He looked at Ling and then announced to the crowd, "Behold, your new emperor, Ling!"

Ling couldn't believe it. Ling couldn't even grow his seed. How could he be the new emperor?

Then the emperor said, "One year ago today, I gave everyone here a seed. I told you to take the seed, plant it, water it and bring it back to me today. But I gave you all boiled seeds which would not grow. All of you, except Ling, have brought me trees and plants and flowers. When you found that the seed would not grow, you substituted another seed for the one I gave you. Ling was the only one with the courage and honesty to bring me a pot with my seed in it. Therefore, he is the one who will be the new emperor!"

Facing Obstacles

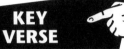**KEY VERSE**

Blessed is the man who perseveres under trial, because when he has stood the test, he will receive the crown of life that God has promised to those who love him.
James 1:12

**APPLICATION**

Face obstacles head on—God often uses the challenging situations in our lives as opportunities to strengthen our faith.

**ADDITIONAL SCRIPTURES**

Joshua 1:9; 1 Chronicles 28:20; Matthew 17:20; James 1:2-4

**ILLUSTRATION**

In ancient times, a king had a boulder placed on a roadway. Then he hid himself and watched to see if anyone would remove the huge rock.

Some of the king's wealthiest merchants and courtiers came by and simply walked around the boulder. Many loudly blamed the king for not keeping the roads clear, but no one did anything to move the stone.

A peasant was traveling on the road carrying a load of vegetables. When he came upon the boulder, the peasant laid down his burden and tried to move the heavy stone to the side of the road. After much pushing and straining, he finally succeeded. As he picked up his load of vegetables to be on his way, the peasant noticed a purse lying in the road where the boulder had been.

Opening the purse, the peasant found many gold coins

and a note from the king indicating that the gold was for the person who removed the boulder from the roadway. The king then came out from his hiding place and congratulated the peasant for passing the test.

The peasant learned what many of us never understand: Every obstacle presents an opportunity to improve our condition.

Fish Feeding

KEY VERSE

But his delight is in the law of the LORD and on his law he meditates day and night. He is like a tree planted by streams of water, which yields its fruit in season and whose leaf does not wither. Whatever he does prospers.
Psalm 1:2-3

APPLICATION

Each of us should make a daily habit of studying the Word of God just like we make a daily habit of eating.

ADDITIONAL SCRIPTURES

Deuteronomy 11:18-23; Psalm 119:9,57-60; 2 Timothy 3:16-17

ILLUSTRATION

It's funny how goldfish eat. If you put too much food in the tank, they'll eat until they explode—and if you put too little, they stop eating all together. You have to be consistent, feeding them the right amount each day in order for them to remain healthy.

We're much the same as goldfish when it comes to God's Word. We need a consistent diet of it every day to stay healthy. It does no good to starve ourselves for a whole year and then gorge for a week on His Word at a camp or on a retreat. And if we don't study God's Word consistently, we won't want it anymore at all.

The Football Game

KEY VERSE

How great is the love the Father has lavished on us, that we should be called children of God! And that is what we are! The reason the world does not know us is that it did not know him.
1 John 3:1

APPLICATION

What a privilege it is to be loved as a father loves his own child by the creator of the world. Is it a privilege you understand and have accepted?

ADDITIONAL SCRIPTURES

Jeremiah 31:3; Luke 11:5-13; Romans 8:31-39; Ephesians 3:16-19; 1 John 3:16-23

ILLUSTRATION

There was a skinny young boy who lived alone with his father and loved football with all his heart. Practice after practice, he eagerly gave everything he had. But being half the size of the other boys, he got absolutely nowhere. At all the games this hopeful athlete sat on the bench and hardly ever played. The young boy and his father had a very special relationship. Even though the son was always on the bench, his father was always in the stands cheering. He never missed a game.

When he entered high school, the young man was still the smallest of the class. Although his father encouraged him to follow his dreams, he also made it very clear that the young man did not have to play football if he didn't

want to. But the young man truly loved football and decided to play. Determined to try his best at every practice, the young man thought that perhaps he'd get to play when he became a senior.

All through his four years of high school, the young man never missed a practice or game; still he remained a benchwarmer and never once got the chance to play in a real game. His faithful father was always in the stands, always with words of encouragement for him.

When the young man went off to college, he decided to try out for the football team as a walk-on. Everyone was sure he could never make the cut, but he did. The coach admitted that he kept him on the roster because the young man always puts his heart and soul into every practice and, at the same time, provided the other players with the spirit and hustle they badly needed. The news that he had survived the cut thrilled him so much that he rushed to the nearest phone and called his father, who shared his excitement. The young man sent season tickets to his father for all the college games in which the young man hardly played.

At the end of his senior football season, as he trotted onto the practice field shortly before the big playoff game, the coach met him with a telegram. As the young man read the words, he became deathly silent. Swallowing hard, he mumbled to the coach, "My father died this morning. Is it all right if I miss practice today?"

The coach put his arm gently around his shoulder and said, "Take the rest of the week off, son. And don't even plan to come back for the game on Saturday."

Saturday arrived, and the game was not going well. In the third quarter, when the team was 10 points behind, a silent young man quietly slipped into the empty locker room and put on his football gear. As he ran onto the sidelines, the coach and his players were astounded to see their faithful teammate back so soon.

"Coach, please let me play," the young man begged. "I've just got to play today."

The coach pretended not to hear him. There was no way he wanted his worst player in this close playoff game. But the young man persisted, and finally feeling sorry for the kid, the coach gave in. "OK, OK," he said. "You can go in."

Before long, the coach, the players and everyone in the stands could not believe their eyes. This little unknown, who had never played before, was doing everything right. The opposing team could not stop him. He ran. He

passed, blocked and tackled like a star. His team began to triumph and the score was soon tied. In the closing seconds of the game, this kid intercepted a pass and ran all the way for the winning touchdown.

The fans went crazy. His teammates hoisted him onto their shoulders. The crowd roared like the team had never heard. Finally, after the stands had emptied and the team had showered and left the locker room, the coach noticed that this young man was sitting quietly in the corner all alone. The coach walked up to him and said, "Kid, I can't believe it. You were fantastic! Tell me what got into you? How did you do it?"

The young man looked at the coach and, with tears in his eyes, said, "Well, Coach, you know that my dad died, but did you also know that my dad was blind?" The young man swallowed hard and forced a smile. "Dad came to all my games, but today was the first time he could see me play, and I wanted to show him I could do it."

Like this athlete's father, God is always there cheering for us. He's always reminding us to go on. He's even offering us His hand, for He knows what is best and is willing to give us what we need—not simply what we want. God has never missed a single game.

What a joy to know that life is meaningful if lived for the Highest. Live for Him as He watches you in the game of life. Amen.

Forgiveness

KEY VERSE

Yet to all who received him, to those who believed in his name, he gave the right to become children of God—children born not of natural descent, nor of human decision or a husband's will, but born of God.
John 1:12-13

APPLICATION

God not only loves us and forgives us, but He also desires for us to be His very own children and to call Him Papa.

ADDITIONAL SCRIPTURES

Psalm 86:5; Jeremiah 31:34; Romans 8:12-17; Galatians 3:26—4:7

ILLUSTRATION

The following is a letter written to a man on death row by the father of the man whom the prisoner had killed:

> You are probably surprised that I, of all people, am writing a letter to you, but I ask you to read it in its entirety and consider its request seriously. As the father of the man whom you took part in murdering, I have something very important to say to you.
>
> I forgive you. With all my heart, I forgive you. I realize it may be hard for you to believe, but I really do. At your trial, when you confessed to your part in the events that cost my son his life and asked for my forgiveness, I immediately granted you that forgiving love from my heart. I can only

hope you believe me and will accept my forgiveness.

But this is not all I have to say to you. I want to make you an offer—I want you to become my adopted child. You see my son who died was my only child, and I now want to share my life with you and leave my riches to you. This may not make sense to you or anyone else, but I believe you are worth the offer. I have arranged matters so that if you will receive my offer of forgiveness, not only will you be pardoned for your crime, but you also will be set free from your imprisonment, and your sentence of death will be dismissed. At that point, you will become my adopted child and heir to all my riches.

I realize this is a risky offer for me to make to you—you might be tempted to reject my offer completely—but I make it to you without reservation.

Also, I realize it may seem foolish to make such an offer to one who cost my son his life, but I now have a great love and an unchangeable forgiveness in my heart for you.

Finally, you may be concerned that once you accept my offer you may do something to cause you to be denied your rights as an heir to my wealth. Nothing could be further from the truth. If I can forgive you for your part in my son's death, I can forgive you for anything. I know you never will be perfect, but you do not have to be perfect to receive my offer. Besides, I believe that once you have accepted my offer and begin to experience the riches that will come to you from me, your primary (though not always) response will be gratitude and loyalty.

Some would call me foolish for my offer to you, but I wish for you to call me your father.

Sincerely,
God

Frederick the Great, King of Prussia

KEY VERSE

If we confess our sins, he is faithful and just and will forgive us our sins and purify us from all unrighteousness.
1 John 1:9

APPLICATION

Do not be afraid to confess your wrongdoings. God will forgive you and set you free from the debt of them.

ADDITIONAL SCRIPTURES

Isaiah 49:8-11; 53:4-11; Zechariah 9:11-12; John 8:31-32; Romans 6:15-23; 1 John 1:7-8,10

ILLUSTRATION

We humans do not like to admit that our sinfulness and rebellion are at the heart of the problems of society. We are much more comfortable discussing imperfections, weaknesses, mistakes and errors in judgment. These terms are socially acceptable, and almost everyone identifies with them. But an outright acknowledgment of guilt before a holy God—complete acceptance of responsibility for wrongdoing—runs against the grain. Yet this kind of honesty is the first step to the freedom from sin and guilt that God longs to give us and has provided in the death of Christ.

The story is told that one day the king of Prussia, Frederick the Great, visited a prison and talked with each of the inmates. There were endless tales of innocence, of misunderstood motives and of exploitation.

Finally, the king stopped at the cell of a convict who remained silent. "Well," remarked Frederick, "I suppose you are an innocent victim too?"

"No, sir, I'm not," replied the man. "I'm guilty and deserve my punishment."

Turning to the warden, the king said, "Here, release this rascal before he corrupts all these fine innocent people in here!"

Getting Knocked Down

KEY VERSE

I have fought the good fight, I have finished the race, I have kept the faith.
2 Timothy 4:7

APPLICATION

In the race of life, run hard toward the finish and no matter what or who knocks you down, keep your eyes on the Lord and you will finish well.

ADDITIONAL SCRIPTURES

Luke 9:61-62; 1 Corinthians 9:24-27; Philippians 3:13-14; 2 Timothy 2:10-13; 1 John 5:4-5

ILLUSTRATION

During a Monday-night football game between the Chicago Bears and the New York Giants, one of the announcers observed that Walter Payton, the Bears' running back, had accumulated over nine miles in career rushing yardage. The other announcer remarked, "Yeah, and that's with someone knocking him down every 4.6 yards!"

Walter Payton, the most successful running back to ever play the game, knew that everyone—even the best—gets knocked down. The key to success is to get up and run again just as hard.

Giving and Receiving–A Circle of Love

KEY VERSE

*A generous man will himself be blessed,
for he shares his food with the poor.*
Proverbs 22:9

APPLICATION

God repays our generosity to others by blessing our lives.

ADDITIONAL SCRIPTURES

Proverbs 11:24-25; Luke 6:38; Acts 20:35; 2 Corinthians 9:5-7; Galatians 6:10

ILLUSTRATION

Every morning on my way to work in downtown Chicago, I encountered a heavyset, middle-aged woman in a shabby coat soliciting spare change in front of an old brick church. She greeted everyone with a smile and a pleasant "Good morning." I always gave her something.

After almost a year of this routine, she disappeared. I wondered what had happened to her. Then one beautiful day, there she was again, in front of the church, wearing the shabby coat.

As I reached into my purse for the usual donation, she stopped me. "Thank you for helping me all those days," she said. "You won't see me again because I've got a job."

With that, she reached into a bag and handed me a wrapped package. She had been standing at her old spot waiting—not for a handout, but for the people she recognized so that she could give each of us a doughnut.

Giving to Others

KEY VERSE

In everything I did, I showed you that by this kind of hard work we must help the weak, remembering the words the Lord Jesus himself said: "It is more blessed to give than to receive."
Acts 20:35

APPLICATION

Regardless of our financial status, whether we are wealthy or poor, there is joy and blessing in giving to meet the needs of others.

ADDITIONAL SCRIPTURES

Isaiah 58:6-8,10; Matthew 25:34-45; Romans 12:20; 2 Corinthians 9:12-14

ILLUSTRATION

Mother Teresa once told the following story:

> One night, a man came to our house to tell me about a family of eight children who had not eaten anything for days. They had nothing to eat. I took enough rice for a meal and went to their house. I could see the hungry faces, the children with their bulging eyes. The sight could not have been more dramatic!
>
> The mother took the rice from my hands, divided it in half and went out. When she came back a little later, I asked her, "Where did you go? What did you do?"
>
> She answered, "They are also hungry."

They were the people next door, a family with the same number of children to feed and who did not have any food either. That mother was aware of the situation. She had the courage and the love to share her meager portion of rice with others. In spite of her circumstances, I think she felt very happy to share with her neighbors the little I had taken her. In order not to take away her happiness, I did not take her any more rice that night. I took her some more the following day.

God's Children Are Heirs

KEY VERSE

Now if we are children, then we are heirs—heirs of God and co-heirs with Christ.
Romans 8:17

APPLICATION

Through Christ's death on the cross, the debt of our sin has been paid in full. Through faith, we become God's children, entitled to the rich inheritance of God's blessings.

ADDITIONAL SCRIPTURES

John 1:12; Galatians 3:1-5,26-29; Ephesians 1:3,7-8,13-14,18-19; Colossians 2:13-14

ILLUSTRATION

There was once a young man who wanted more than anything to take a cruise aboard a luxury liner. He did not have much money, but eventually the young man saved enough to purchase a ticket.

As he packed, the young man knew he would be traveling with no money for food, so he carefully packed some bread and cheese for his meals. Although he truly enjoyed the cruise, as he walked around and watched people eating in the dining and banquet halls of the ship, his joy diminished.

After two weeks, his bread and cheese molding, the young man was starving. As he walked around, people noticed how painfully thin he had become. A gentleman approached and asked the young man if there was anything wrong. Slightly embarrassed, the young man

explained that he did not have enough money for food. The gentleman took the young man by the shoulders and explained to him that the food was all paid for in the price of the ticket. The young man was astonished—all this time he could have been eating at the wonderful banquets, but he hadn't known it!

Many Christians do not realize that they are coheirs with Christ—children of the King—and just as this young man, they walk through life missing out on all the King has provided. There is a heavenly banquet waiting for us. Jesus paid the entire cost for us; all we have to do is accept His invitation to join Him!

God's Strength Through Our Weakness

KEY VERSE

But he said to me, "My grace is sufficient for you, for my power is made perfect in weakness." Therefore I will boast all the more gladly about my weaknesses, so that Christ's power may rest on me. That is why, for Christ's sake, I delight in weaknesses, in insults, in hardships, in persecutions, in difficulties. For when I am weak, then I am strong.
2 Corinthians 12:9-10

APPLICATION

By facing weaknesses realistically, we recognize our need for God and for His power to work through us.

ADDITIONAL SCRIPTURES

Psalm 28:8; 1 Corinthians 2:3-5; 2 Corinthians 13:4; Hebrews 11:32-34; James 1:2-5

ILLUSTRATION

I asked God for strength, that I might achieve.
I was made weak, that I might learn humbly to obey.
I asked for health, that I might do great things.
I was given infirmity, that I might do better things.
I asked for riches, that I might be happy.
I was given poverty, that I might be wise.

I asked for power, that I might have the praise of men.

I was given weakness, that I might feel the need of God.

I asked for all things, that I might enjoy life.

I was given life, that I might enjoy all things.

I got nothing I asked for—but everything I had hoped for.

Almost despite myself, my unspoken prayers were answered.

I am, among men, most richly blessed!

—Unidentified Confederate soldier

High-Dive Conversion

KEY VERSE

For God was pleased to have all his fullness dwell in him, and through him to reconcile to himself all things, whether things on earth or things in heaven, by making peace through his blood, shed on the cross.

Once you were alienated from God and were enemies in your minds because of your evil behavior. But now he has reconciled you by Christ's physical body through death to present you holy in his sight, without blemish and free from accusation.
Colossians 1:19-22

APPLICATION

Jesus' death on the cross provided the ultimate power to forgive our sins and to reconcile us to God.

ADDITIONAL SCRIPTURES

Romans 5:10; 1 Corinthians 1:17-18; Ephesians 1:7; 2:13; Revelation 1:5

ILLUSTRATION

In 1967, while taking a class in photography at the University of Cincinnati, I became acquainted with a young man named Charles Murray, a fellow student at the school, training as a high diver for the summer Olympics of 1968.

Charles was very patient with me as I would speak to him for hours about Jesus Christ and how He had saved me. Charles was not raised in a home that attended any kind of church, so all that I had told him was a fascination

to him. He even began to ask questions about forgiveness of sin. Finally the day came that I put a question to him. I asked if he realized his own need of a redeemer and if he was ready to trust Christ as his own Savior. I saw his countenance fall and the guilt in his face. His reply was a strong no.

In the days that followed, Charles was quiet and often I felt that he was avoiding me. Finally, he called and wanted to know where to look in the New Testament for some verses I had given him about salvation. I gave him the references to several passages and asked if I could meet with him. He declined my offer and thanked me for the Scripture. I could tell that he was greatly troubled, but I did not know where he was or how to help him.

Because he was training for the Olympic games, Charles had special privileges at the university pool facilities. Sometime between 10:30 and 11:00 that evening he decided to swim and practice a few dives. It was a clear night in October and the moon was big and bright. The university pool was housed under a ceiling of glass panes, so the moon shone brightly across the top of the wall in the pool area. Charles climbed to the highest platform to take his first dive. At that moment the Spirit of God began to convict him of his sins. All the Scripture he had read, all the occasions of my witnessing to him about Christ flooded his mind. As he prepared to make his dive, he stood backwards on the platform, spread his arms to gather his balance and looked up to the wall, where he saw his own shadow caused by the light of the moon. It was the shape of a cross. He could bear the burden of his sin no longer. His heart broke, and he sat down on the platform suspended 20 feet in the air and asked God to forgive him.

Suddenly, the lights in the pool area came on. The attendant had come in to check the pool. As Charles looked down from his platform, he saw that the pool was empty; it had been drained for repairs. He had almost plummeted to his death, but the Cross had kept him from disaster.

Contributed by
Doug Webster

How Do You Live Your Dash?

KEY VERSE

I urge you to live a life worthy of the calling you have received.
Ephesians 4:1

APPLICATION

Have you lived a life worthy of the calling you have received? We are called to spend our dash living holy lives as an example to others.

ADDITIONAL SCRIPTURES

Ephesians 4:2-3; 1 Timothy 4:12; James 3:13; 1 Peter 4:1-6; 1 John 2:17

ILLUSTRATION

A pastor stood to speak
At the funeral of his friend.
He referred to the dates on her tombstone
From the beginning to the end.
He noted that first came the date of her birth
And spoke of the second date with tears,
But he said what mattered most of all
Was the dash between those years.
For that dash represents all the time
That she spent alive on earth.
And now only those who loved her
Know what that little dash is worth.
For it matters not how much we own—
The cars, the house, the cash.
What matters most is how we live
And how we spend our dash.
So think about this long and hard,

Illustrations and Stories

Are there things you'd like to change?
For you never know what time is left;
You could be at "dash, midrange."
If we could just slow down enough
To see what's true and real,
And always try to understand
The way that others feel.
And be less quick to anger,
And show appreciation more,
And love the people in our lives
Like we've never loved before.
If we treat each other with respect
And more often wear a smile,
Keeping in mind this special dash
Might last but a short while.
So when your eulogy's being read,
Your life's actions to rehash,
Would you smile at the things being said
About how you spent your little dash?

Letter from a Friend

KEY VERSE

For since the creation of the world God's invisible qualities—his eternal power and divine nature— have been clearly seen, being understood from what has been made, so that men are without excuse.
Romans 1:20

APPLICATION

God reveals Himself in His creation. Look around you and see how He is revealing Himself to you today.

ADDITIONAL SCRIPTURES

Genesis 1:1-38; Psalm 136; Romans 1:19

ILLUSTRATION

Dear Child,

I am writing to say how much I care for you and to say how much I want you to know Me better. When you awoke this morning, I exploded a brilliant sunrise through your window, hoping to get your attention; but you rushed off without even noticing.

Later, I noticed you were walking with some friends, so I bathed you in warm sunshine and perfumed the air with nature's sweet scent; and still you didn't notice Me. As you passed by, I shouted to you in a thunderstorm and painted a beautiful rainbow in the sky and you didn't even look.

In the evening, I spilled moonlight onto your face and sent a cool breeze to rest you. As you slept, I watched over you and shared your thoughts, but you were unaware that I was so near.

I have chosen you and hope you will talk to Me soon. Until then I will remain near. I am your friend, and I love you very much.

Your friend,
Jesus

Letter from Sister Mary Rose

KEY VERSE

Hatred stirs up dissension, but love covers over all wrongs.
Proverbs 10:12

APPLICATION

Our words can impact a life in ways beyond our imagination. A little girl, abandoned by her mother, heard the words "I love you" and it changed everything. Remember to speak words of encouragement and love to your friends and family.

ADDITIONAL SCRIPTURES

Proverbs 29:15; Matthew 5:43-44; 1 Thessalonians 2:7-8; 5:11; 1 John 4:7-8

ILLUSTRATION

The following story is true:

Dear Friend,

She came to our front door Tuesday morning, dressed in dirty rags, holding a little aluminum paint can in her arms.

From the second she stepped inside our shelter, she mystified us. Whatever she did, wherever she went, the paint can never left her hands.

When Kathy sat in the crisis shelter, the can sat in her arms. She took the can with her to the cafe-

teria that first morning she ate and to bed with her that first night she slept.

When she stepped into the shower, the can was only a few feet away. When the tiny homeless girl dressed, the can rested alongside her feet.

"I'm sorry, this is mine," she told our counselors whenever we asked her about it. "This can belongs to me."

"Do you want to tell me what's in it, Kathy?" I'd ask her.

"Um, not today," she would reply. "Not today."

When Kathy was sad or angry or hurt—which happened a lot—she took her paint can to a quiet dorm room on the third floor. Many times on Tuesday, Wednesday and Thursday of each week, I'd pass by her room and watch her rock gently back and forth, the can in her arms. Sometimes she'd even talk to the paint can in low whispers.

I've been around troubled kids all my life—over 41,000 homeless kids will come to our shelters this year! I'm used to seeing them carry stuffed animals—some of the roughest, toughest kids at Covenant House have a stuffed animal. Every kid has something—needs something—to hold.

But a paint can? I could feel alarm bells ringing in my head.

Early this morning, I decided to accidentally run into her again. "Would you like to join me for breakfast?" I said.

"That would be great," she said.

For a few minutes we sat in a corner of our cafeteria, talking quietly over the din of 150 ravenous homeless kids. Then I took a deep breath and plunged into it.

"Kathy, that's a really nice can. What's in it?"

For a long time, Kathy didn't answer. She rocked back and forth, her hair swaying across her shoulders. Then she looked over at me, tears in her eyes.

"It's my mother," she said.

"Oh. What do you mean, it's your mother?" I asked.

"It's my mother's ashes," she said. "I went and got them from the funeral home. See, I even asked them to put a label right here on the side. It has her name on it."

Kathy held the can up before my eyes. A little label on the side chronicled all that remained of her mother: her date of birth, her date of death and her name. That was it. Then Kathy pulled the can close and hugged it.

"I never really knew my mother, Sister," Kathy told me. "I mean, she threw me in the garbage two days after I was born." We checked Kathy's story. Sure enough, the year Kathy was born, the New York newspapers ran a story saying that police had found a little infant girl in a dumpster—and yes, it was two days after Kathy was born.

"I ended up living in a lot of foster homes, and I was really mad at my mother," Kathy said. "But then I decided I was going to try to find her. I got lucky—someone knew where she was living. I went to her house."

"She wasn't there, Sister," she said. "My mother was in the hospital. She had AIDS. She was dying."

"I went to the hospital, and I got to meet her the day before she died. My mother told me she loved me, Sister," Kathy said crying. "She told me she loved me." We double-checked Kathy's story—every word of it was true.

I reached out and hugged Kathy, and she cried in my arms for a long, long time. It was tough getting my arms around her, because she just would not put the paint can down. But she didn't seem to mind. I know I didn't.

—Sister Mary Rose
President
Covenant House
California

Eric Liddell

KEY VERSE

Then he said to them all: "If anyone would come after me, he must deny himself and take up his cross daily and follow me. For whoever wants to save his life will lose it, but whoever loses his life for me will save it."
Luke 9:23-24

APPLICATION

You will have to deny yourself a lot of what you want and take some big risks to live and follow Jesus as a true disciple. Matthew 16:24-28; Mark 8:34-38; Luke 9:18-22,25-27;

ADDITIONAL SCRIPTURES

Galatians 2:20; Philippians 1:21; 2 Timothy 2:11-13

ILLUSTRATION

When a major production company in Britain decided to do a film about an athlete of the 1920s, media experts predicted they would lose millions. But it turned out the picture became an Academy Award winner, and *Chariots of Fire* roused a hero worship that the experts did not know was still there.

As good as the picture is, however, it falls short of actually demonstrating how great a man Eric Liddell really was, not in the sense of being a great athlete, but in the larger sense of being a man great in character and integrity. *Chariots of Fire* focused on the contests that took Liddell to the 1924 Olympics in Paris, where his conviction kept him from running the 100-meter race—his specialty—because it was held on a Sunday. Instead, Liddell chose to run in the 400-meter race and was further hand-

icapped because he drew an outside lane where there were no other runners to help him set his pace. Liddell, of course, raced to victory and later returned to his native city of Edinburgh, Scotland, as a great hero.

The story of Eric Liddell's life, however, had just begun at that point. Turning his back on a life as an international hero and one of Scotland's favorite sons, Liddell chose to follow in the steps of his father and became a missionary to China. In 1925, Liddell left for China to begin missionary work at the Anglo-Chinese Christian College. Although Liddell ran some, the Chinese could not quite understand the strange Anglo-Saxon who ran through the crowded streets; and since it was not culturally very acceptable to the Chinese, Liddell stopped running. He did, however, accept an invitation to Japan three years later in 1928 to run in a 400-meter international event. Running in his own unique style, Liddell outclassed his opponents and swept the field, to the delight of the Japanese crowd.

What the crowd did not know was that Liddell's ship back to China was due to leave 15 minutes after the event. At the finish line, Liddell mystified officials and spectators alike by continuing to run on under the grandstand and out of the stadium to a waiting taxi that rushed Liddell to the docks. The ship had already cast off from the jetty. In a final sprint, Liddell ran down the pier and leaped to the decks of the ship 15 feet away.

Ironically, Liddell spent his last days with the Japanese—not as a guest, but as a prisoner. When the Japanese invasion of China seemed imminent, Liddell sent his family home but remained behind to work as a missionary. He was soon arrested and placed in a Japanese prisoner-of-war camp. A man who knew Liddell in the concentration camp wrote the following:

> For Eric Liddell, death came just a few months before liberation. He was buried in the little cemetery in the part of the camp where others who had died during internment had been laid to rest. I remember being part of the honor guard made up of children from the Chefoo and Weihsein Schools. None of us will ever forget this man who was totally committed to putting God first; a man whose humble life combined muscular Christianity with radiant godliness.

What was his secret? He unreservedly committed his life to Jesus Christ as his Savior and Lord. That friendship meant everything to him. By the flickering light of a peanut-oil lamp early each morning, he studied the Bible and talked with God for an hour every day. As a Christian, Eric Liddell's desire was to know God more deeply and, as a missionary, to make Him known more fully. That is the real story of Eric Liddell's greatness.

The Little Boy Who Wanted to Fight Fires

KEY VERSE

I press on toward the goal to win the prize for which God has called me heavenward in Christ Jesus.
Philippians 3:14

APPLICATION

Don't allow fear and other doubts to keep you from living out your life passionately for the Lord Jesus.

ADDITIONAL SCRIPTURES

Luke 9:61-62; Philippians 3:12-13,15-16; 1 Timothy 1:6-7

ILLUSTRATION

Once there was a little boy who, ever since he could remember, wanted to be a fireman. The shrill of the siren and the deep rumble of the racing fire truck had filled his dreams almost every night. Deep in his heart there was a longing to someday be able to help people, to save people from the ravaging grasp of a fire. It was not the whim of childhood fantasy; his was the unmistakable call of destiny.

Growing up never changed his mind.

To be sure, he had gone through all the indecisions and doubts of adolescence, the well-meaning questions of friends and family who "wondered whether he could be happy as a fireman." But he never wavered. He was meant to be a fireman. He was meant to put out fires.

Oh, how he longed for the day when he would no

longer be a spectator but could participate actively as a firefighter.

Finally the big day when he could take the first real step to fulfill his lifelong dream arrived: He was accepted at one of the best firefighter schools in the country. His teachers were world renowned. For three years he immersed himself in his schooling. He spent hours honing his skills on practice fires. He studied firefighting theory long into the nights.

Still, after all these years, he had never fought a real fire. As graduation approached, however, he realized that long-awaited moment was within reach.

Suddenly, he began to have doubts. For the first time in his life, he was unsure, afraid and, worse yet, questioning whether he ought to be a fireman at all.

It was then that one of his professors suggested he travel to Europe and study under one of the greatest fireman theorists of all time. He would be recommended by his professors and would receive the finest training available. It would last for two years.

The not-so-little boy decided to travel to Europe and for two years, he exhausted himself in dedicated study and became one of the most brilliantly educated firemen in the world. But all he had ever done was put out practice fires. Once again, graduation loomed before him, and once again he was haunted by indecision. He knew all about fires and could tell anyone how to fight one; in fact, he knew so much, he began to feel that his superior knowledge did, in fact, place him a notch above ordinary firemen. He became increasingly concerned that he might have to fight fires with uneducated firemen, which could result in him being exposed to unnecessary danger.

It was then that he was offered a position to teach at one of the most respected fireman schools in the country. He accepted and for 25 years he taught with honor, receiving worldwide recognition. When he died sometime later, someone found the memoirs he had written on his deathbed. In them was this strange passage:

> I lie here today reviewing my life. I still remember my dream, my passion to be a fireman. More than anything else I wanted to put out fires, but I realized something today. I have never put out a real fire. Never.

—Mike Yaconelli
Youth Specialties

Littleton's Martyrs

KEY VERSE

For to me, to live is Christ and to die is gain.
Philippians 1:21

APPLICATION

As Christians we are to live Christ daily. We can do that without fear because of what Christ did for us.

ADDITIONAL SCRIPTURES

Matthew 25:23; 26:13; Luke 9:23-27; Romans 1:16-17; 12:1; Hebrews 12:1-13

ILLUSTRATION

The following essay was adapted from Charles W. Colson, *Breakpoint Commentary*, April 26, 1999:

It is a test all of us would hope to pass, but none of us really wants to take. A masked gunman pointed his weapon at a Christian and asked, "Do you believe in God?"

She knew that if she said yes, she'd likely pay with her life, but unfaithfulness to her Lord was unthinkable. With what would be her last words, she calmly answered, "Yes, I believe in God."

What makes this story remarkable is that the gunman was no communist thug, nor was the martyr a Chinese pastor. As you may have guessed, the event I am talking about occurred last Tuesday, in Littleton, Colorado.

As the *Washington Post* reported, the two students who shot 13 people, Eric Harris and Dylan Klebold, did not choose their victims at random; they

were acting out a kaleidoscope of ugly prejudices.

Media coverage has centered on the killers' hostility toward racial minorities and athletes, but there was another group the pair hated every bit as much, if not more: Christians. And there were plenty of them to hate at Columbine High School. According to some accounts, eight Christians—four evangelicals and four Catholics—were killed.

Among them was Cassie Bernall. And it was Cassie who made the dramatic decision that I have just described—fitting for a person whose favorite movie was *Braveheart*, in which the hero dies a martyr's death.

Cassie was a 17-year-old junior with long blonde hair—hair she wanted to have cut off and made into wigs for cancer patients who had lost their hair through chemotherapy. She was active in her youth group at Westpool's community church and was known for carrying a Bible to school.

Cassie was in the school library reading her Bible when the two young killers burst in. According to witnesses, one of the killers pointed his gun at Cassie and asked, "Do you believe in God?"

Cassie paused and then answered, "Yes, I believe in God."

"Why?" the gunman asked. Cassie did not have a chance to respond; the gunman had already shot her dead.

As her classmate Mickie Cain told Larry King on CNN, "She completely stood up for God. When the killers asked her if there was anyone who had faith in Christ, she spoke up, and they shot her for it."

Cassie's martyrdom was even more remarkable when you consider that just a few years ago she had dabbled in the occult, including witchcraft. She had embraced the same darkness and nihilism that drove her killers to such despicable acts. But two years prior to her murder, Cassie had dedicated her life to Christ and turned her life around. Her friend Craig Moon called her a "light for Christ."

Well this "light for Christ" became a rare American martyr of the twentieth century. According to the *Boston Globe*, on the night of her death, Cassie's brother Chris found a poem she had written just two days prior to her death. It

read: "Now I have given up on everything else, I have found it to be the only way to really know Christ and to experience the mighty power that brought Him back to life again, and to find out what it means to suffer and to die with Him. So, whatever it takes, I will be the one who lives in the fresh newness of life of those who are alive from the dead."

The best way all of us can honor Cassie's memory is to embrace that same courageous commitment to our faith. We should stand up to our kids when they want to play violent video games. We should be willing to stand up to community ridicule when we oppose access to Internet pornography at the local library.

For the families of these young martyrs, I can only offer deep personal sympathy and hope that they might take strength from the words Jesus spoke to the woman who honored Him by pouring ointment on His head. "Wherever this gospel is preached throughout the world, what she has done will also be told, in memory of her" (Matthew 26:13).

"Well done, good and faithful servant! . . . Come and share your master's happiness!" (Matthew 25:23).

He is no fool who gives up what he cannot keep, to gain what he cannot lose.
—Jim Elliot

I have held many things in my hands, and have lost them all; but whatever I have placed in God's hands, that I still possess.
—Martin Luther

Illustrations and Stories

Lost in the Desert

KEY VERSE

Now faith is being sure of what we hope for and certain of what we do not see.
Hebrews 11:1

APPLICATION

When we trust God and take the chance of relying on Him, He will bless us beyond what we can see with our human perspective. Faith can move mountains.

ADDITIONAL SCRIPTURES

Proverbs 3:5; Matthew 17:19-21; Luke 18:40-42; John 20:29; 1 Timothy 4:12

ILLUSTRATION

Legend has it that a man was lost in the desert, dying for a drink of water. He stumbled upon an old shack—a ramshackle, windowless, roofless, weather-beaten old shack. He looked about this place and found a little shade from the heat of the desert sun. As he glanced around, he saw an old, rusty water pump about 15 feet away. He stumbled over to it, grabbed the handle and began to pump up and down, up and down. Nothing came out.

Disappointed, he staggered back. He noticed off to the side an old jug. He looked at it, wiped away the dirt and dust and read the message written on it: "You have to prime the pump with all the water in this jug, my friend. P.S. Be sure you fill the jug again before you leave."

He popped the cork out of the jug and sure enough, there was water. It was almost full of water! Suddenly, he was faced with a decision. If he drank the water, he could

live. Ah, but if he poured all the water in the old rusty pump, maybe it would yield fresh, cool water from deep down in the well—all the water he wanted.

He studied both options. What should he do—pour it into the old pump and take a chance on fresh, cool water or drink what was in the jug and ignore its message? Should he waste all the water on the hope of those flimsy instructions written no telling how long ago?

Reluctantly he poured all the water into the pump. Then he grabbed the handle and began to pump. Squeak, squeak, squeak. Still, nothing came out! Squeak, squeak, squeak. A little bit began to dribble out, then a small stream flowed, and finally it gushed! To his relief fresh, cool water poured out of the rusty pump. Eagerly, he filled the jug and drank its refreshing contents.

Then he filled the jug for the next traveler. He filled it to the top, popped the cork back on and added these words to the little note: "Believe me, it really works. You have to give it all away before you can get anything back."

People who risk living like that really soar.

Mathilde

KEY VERSE

Am I now trying to win the approval of men, or of God? Or am I trying to please men? If I were still trying to please men, I would not be a servant of Christ.
Galatians 1:10

APPLICATION

Who are you trying to please—man or God? Remember, it *does* matter from which audience you want the applause.

ADDITIONAL SCRIPTURES

Matthew 6:1-4; Acts 5:1-11; Romans 12:9

ILLUSTRATION

There was once a young French woman named Mathilde who desperately wanted to be accepted by high society. Her husband was a common worker, but they managed to be invited to an elegant ball. Mathilde, feeling that she had to make an impression on the people at the ball, borrowed a beautiful necklace to wear from a wealthy friend. She was well accepted by the high-class people at the ball and the evening would have been a total success if it had not been for one small problem: Mathilde lost the borrowed necklace. To keep from having to tell her wealthy friend and risk certain embarrassment, she talked her husband into replacing it. Her husband had to borrow nearly 40,000 francs from every possible source that he knew just to pay for the replacement. Mathilde gave the

replacement to her friend without telling her what had happened.

Mathilde and her husband both worked two jobs to pay back the money they had borrowed to replace the necklace. They had to sell their home and live in a slum. Finally, after 10 long years, Mathilde and her husband were able to pay the last of their debt.

One day, Mathilde ran into the wealthy friend who had loaned her the necklace. The woman hardly recognized Mathilde because she looked so haggard from all the hard work. Mathilde confessed to the wealthy woman that she had lost the borrowed necklace and had had to work very hard to pay for its replacement. The wealthy woman shook her head and explained to Mathilde that the original had been made of fake gemstones, not of real diamonds; it was worth less than 50 francs.

Mathilde and her husband had worked and suffered all those years simply because Mathilde had tried to keep up appearances.

Momentary Pleasures, Lasting Pain

KEY VERSE

[Moses] chose to be mistreated along with the people of God rather than to enjoy the pleasures of sin for a short time. He regarded disgrace for the sake of Christ as of greater value than the treasures of Egypt, because he was looking ahead to his reward.
Hebrews 11:25-26

APPLICATION

Sin can be fun for a while, but in the end it hurts our relationships with God, the people we love and even ourselves.

ADDITIONAL SCRIPTURES

Proverbs 7; 14:12; 1 Corinthians 6:18; Hebrews 3:13; 1 Peter 3:10

ILLUSTRATION

The following letter was written anonymously to the syndicated advice columnist Abigail Van Buren:

Dear Abby,

I can answer the letter from "Upset and Impatient," the married woman who was waiting for her married lover to leave his wife.

I cheated on my wife for years; then, about 10 years ago, I had an affair with a woman and we fell in love. When you are "running around," it's always

under ideal conditions for a short period of time. Everything is well planned, and you always look your best. It's romantic, forbidden and exciting.

But we really didn't know each other.

The love we thought we couldn't live without destroyed our lives and caused untold pain to our families. We gave up our children, our careers and our homes for a marriage that lasted three years.

Since that time, I have remarried. This wonderful woman has taught me how to be faithful to her and to myself. My daughter lives with us and she has forgiven me, but she has not forgotten. My son, who is younger, still carries scars from neglect.

I have spent more time trying to repair what I messed up than I ever have enjoying myself. When people cheat, the pain they cause is always greater than the pleasure they get. Please tell your reader this.

The Most Caring Child

KEY VERSE

Praise be to the God and Father of our Lord Jesus Christ, the Father of compassion and the God of all comfort, who comforts us in all our troubles, so that we can comfort those in any trouble with the comfort we ourselves have received from God.
2 Corinthians 1:3-4

APPLICATION

Those who have been comforted by God should comfort others in their time of need.

ADDITIONAL SCRIPTURES

Psalm 40:1-3; 91:1-6; Isaiah 51:12; Micah 6:8

ILLUSTRATION

Author and lecturer Leo Buscaglia once talked about a contest he was asked to judge. The purpose of the contest was to find the most caring child. The winner was a four-year-old child whose next-door neighbor was an elderly gentleman who had recently lost his wife. Upon seeing the man cry, the little boy went into the old gentleman's yard, climbed onto his lap and just sat there. When his mother asked him what he had said to the neighbor, the little boy said, "Nothing. I just helped him cry."

No Favoritism Allowed

KEY VERSE

*Do not pervert justice; do not show partiality to
the poor or favoritism to the great, but
judge your neighbor fairly.*
Leviticus 19:15

APPLICATION

We are called to treat people lovingly and respectful-
ly—without playing favorites. We are to love others as
God loves us—for who we are, not for our beauty, wealth
or behavior.

**ADDITIONAL
SCRIPTURES**

1 Samuel 16:7; Romans 12:9-10; James 2:1-9; 1 Peter
3:3-4

ILLUSTRATION

To feel disgust at times is quite natural. The virtue—which
at times is of heroic proportions—is found in being able
to overcome disgust for the love of Jesus. This is the secret
we discover in the lives of some saints: the ability to go
beyond what is merely natural.

Saint Francis of Assisi once ran into a leper who was
completely disfigured. Naturally, he was disgusted and
instinctively backed up. Then, realizing his reaction, he
overcame the disgust he felt and kissed the face that had
repelled him.

What was the outcome of this? Francis became filled
with tremendous joy. And the leper? He went on his way,
praising God as he went.

Illustrations and Stories

Observation Is the Key

KEY VERSE

Dear friends, do not believe every spirit, but test the spirits to see whether they are from God, because many false prophets have gone out into the world.
1 John 4:1

APPLICATION

You cannot believe everything you hear no matter who tells you. Test against the Word of God what people tell you and then judge for the truth.

ADDITIONAL SCRIPTURES

John 8:31-32; 1 Corinthians 2:6-16; 1 John 4:2-6

ILLUSTRATION

At a prestigious Ivy League medical school the new medical students were starting their first day of classes. They were all a little nervous because the professor also happened to be the dean of the medical department. As he entered the room, everyone became quiet and prepared to write down every word the professor uttered.

"Observation is the key to medicine," he began. Students began writing furiously. From out of his briefcase the professor produced a small test tube of yellow liquid and continued, "This is human urine. Many times, patients' conditions can be determined by observing the contents of their urine. How it smells and tastes can often be enough to let you know what's wrong." At this, the professor dipped a finger into the urine and into his mouth. The students were shocked—and even more so

when the professor passed the test tube down the rows of students, instructing them to do as he had done.

One by one, students placed their fingers into the urine and tasted it. There were many scowls and groans as the test tube made it to the last student and finally back to the professor, who held up the tube and concluded, "You have just had your first lesson in observing. For if you had observed a little closer, you would have seen that I had put my index finger into the urine and my middle finger into my mouth."

The Poison Tongue

KEY VERSE

With the tongue we praise our Lord and Father, and with it we curse men, who have been made in God's likeness. Out of the same mouth come praise and cursing. My brothers, this should not be.
James 3:9-10

APPLICATION

Our words have the power to either build others up or tear them down. Our words reflect the condition of our hearts. Christ's followers are called to speak blessings, not curses.

ADDITIONAL SCRIPTURES

Proverbs 12:18; 16:23-24; Matthew 12:34-36; 15:18; Ephesians 4:29; James 3:3-8,11-12

ILLUSTRATION

There was once an extremely courageous woman—courageous for several reasons, including her uphill battle against alcoholism and her resolve to do all she could to restore her relationship with God. It's tough to start over—it's even tougher when people won't let you.

The woman chose a small church to attend, one where she knew many members and believed she would be received with open arms. On the Sunday she decided to attend, she parked her car near the church building and got out. As she walked toward the front door, she over-heard two ladies talking nearby. The stinging words were not meant for her ears, but she heard them anyway.

"How long is that alcoholic going to hang around here?" she heard one of them say.

The woman turned and walked sadly back to her car. She never again entered a church building until she died and her funeral was held in one.

Those ladies at the church that day meant no harm, yet gossip is never innocent—and it can do irreparable damage.

The Power of Encouragement

KEY VERSE

Therefore encourage one another and build each other up, just as in fact you are doing.
1 Thessalonians 5:11

APPLICATION

Encouragement is the vital component for building up and strengthening others in faith. We can change lives through our affirmation!

ADDITIONAL SCRIPTURES

Acts 11:23; 15:32; Romans 1:12; 15:2; Ephesians 4:29; 1 Thessalonians 3:2; 2 Timothy 4:2; Hebrews 3:13; 10:25

ILLUSTRATION

He was in the third-grade class I taught at St. Mary's school in Morris, Minnesota. All of my students were very dear to me, but Mark Eklund was one in a million. He was very neat in appearance and had that happy-to-be-alive attitude that made even his occasional mischievousness delightful.

Mark talked incessantly. I had to remind him again and again that talking without permission was not acceptable. What impressed me so much, though, was his sincere response every time I had to correct him for misbehaving. "Thank you for correcting me, Sister," he would say. I didn't know what to make of it at first, but before long I became accustomed to hearing it many times each day.

One morning my patience was growing thin when Mark talked once too often, and then I made a novice teacher's mistake. I looked at him and said, "If you say one more word, I am going to tape your mouth shut!"

It wasn't 10 seconds later that Chuck blurted out, "Mark is talking again."

I hadn't asked any students to help me watch Mark, but since I had stated the punishment in front of the class, I had to act on it.

I remember the scene as if it were yesterday. I walked to my desk, very deliberately opened the desk drawer and took out a roll of masking tape. Without saying a word I proceeded to Mark's desk, tore off two pieces of tape and made a big *X* with them over his mouth. I then returned to the front of the room. As I glanced at Mark to see how he was doing, he winked at me. That did it. I started laughing. The class cheered as I walked back to Mark's desk, removed the tape and shrugged my shoulders. His first words were, "Thank you for correcting me, Sister."

At the end of the year I was asked to teach high school math. The years flew by, and before I knew it Mark was in my classroom again. He was more handsome than ever and just as polite. Since he had to listen carefully to my instruction in the "new math," he did not talk as much in ninth grade as he had in the third.

One Friday, things just didn't feel right. We had worked hard on a new concept all week, and I sensed that the students were frowning and frustrated with themselves, and they were edgy with one another. I felt I had to stop this crankiness before it got out of hand. So I asked them to list the names of all their fellow students in the room on two sheets of paper leaving space between each name.

Then I told them to think of the nicest thing they could say about each classmate and write it down. It took the remainder of the class period to finish the assignment, and as the students left the room, each one handed me their papers. Charlie smiled. Mark said, "Thank you for teaching me, Sister. Have a good weekend."

That Saturday, I wrote down the name of each student on a separate sheet of paper, and I listed what everyone else had said about that individual. On Monday I gave each student his or her list. Before long the entire class was smiling. "I never knew others liked me so much," I heard whispered around.

No one ever mentioned those papers again in class. I

never knew whether they discussed them after class or shared them with their parents, but it didn't matter. The exercise had accomplished its purpose. The students were happy with themselves and one another once again.

That group of students moved on. Several years later, after I returned from vacation, my parents met me at the airport. As we were driving home my mother asked me the usual questions about the trip, the weather, etc. Then she gave Dad a sideways glance and simply said, "Dad?"

My father cleared his throat as he usually did before something important. "The Eklunds called last night," he began. "Mark was killed in Vietnam. The funeral is tomorrow, and his parents would like you to attend." I can still remember the exact spot on I-494 where Dad told me about Mark.

I had never seen a serviceman in a military coffin before. Mark looked so handsome, so mature. All I could think of at that moment was, *Mark, I would give all the masking tape in the world if only you would talk to me.*

The church was packed with Mark's friends. Chuck's sister sang. Why did it have to rain on the day of the funeral? It was difficult enough at the graveside. The pastor said the usual prayers and the bugler played taps. One by one, those who loved Mark took a last walk by the coffin. I was the last one.

As I stood there, one of the soldiers who had acted as a pallbearer came up to me. "Were you Mark's math teacher?" he asked.

I nodded as I continued to stare at the coffin.

"Mark talked about you a lot," he said.

After the funeral most of Mark's former classmates headed for Chuck's farmhouse for lunch. Mark's mother and father were there, wanting to talk with me. "We want to show you something," his father said, taking a wallet out of his pocket. "They found this on Mark when he was killed. We thought you might recognize it."

Opening the billfold, he carefully removed two worn pieces of paper that had obviously been taped, folded and refolded many times. I knew without looking at them that they were the pieces of the paper on which I had listed all the good things Mark's classmates had said about him. "Thank you so much for doing that," Mark's mother said. "As you can see, Mark treasured this."

Mark's classmates gathered around us. Charlie smiled rather sheepishly and said, "I still have my list too. It's in the top drawer of my desk at home."

Chuck's wife said, "Chuck asked me to keep his in our wedding album."

"I have mine too," Marilyn said. Then another class-mate named Vicki reached into her pocketbook and took out her wallet and showed her worn and tattered list to the group. "I carry this with me all the time," she said without batting an eyelash. "I think we all saved our lists."

That's when I finally sat down and cried. I cried for Mark and all his friends who would never see him again.

What a great lesson on what encouraging someone else does. How meaningful it is to say or write something positive to someone. You may never know how far-reaching such an encouragement might be!

—Sister Helen P. Mrosia

The Power of Hope

KEY VERSE

Find rest, O my soul, in God alone; my hope comes from him. He alone is my rock and my salvation; he is my fortress, I will not be shaken.
Psalm 62:5-6

APPLICATION

Hope is a powerful force within us. When our hope is placed in God we are empowered to withstand any trial that may come our way!

ADDITIONAL SCRIPTURES

Proverbs 13:12; Isaiah 40:31; John 14:3; Romans 5:1-5; 15:4; 1 Thessalonians 1:3,5; 4:17

ILLUSTRATION

Several years ago, millionaire Eugene Lang was asked to speak to a class of sixth graders from East Harlem, New York. What could he say to inspire these students, most of whom he knew would drop out of school? Scrapping his notes, he decided to speak to them from his heart. "Stay in school," he admonished, "and I'll help pay the college tuition for every one of you."

That was a turning point. For the first time in their lives, these students had hope. One said, "I had something to look forward to—something waiting for me. It was a golden feeling." Nearly 90 percent of that class went on to graduate from high school.

People without hope are people without a future. But when hope is restored, life is restored. This is especially true for those who come to know Christ. He gives a sure

basis for hope. He has promised to return to Earth to take us to our eternal home (see John 14:3; 1 Thessalonians 4:17). Until then, there is help through the power of the Holy Spirit (see 1 Thessalonians 1:5). The believer experiences a new kind of life now and anticipates its fulfillment when Jesus returns.

Is that hope alive in your heart? If not, admit that you are a sinner. Trust in Christ as your Savior. And He'll give you a hope that makes life worth living.

If Christ lives in your heart, you have a living hope.

The Power of Prayer

KEY VERSE

Trust in the LORD with all your heart and lean not on your own understanding; in all your ways acknowledge him, and he will make your paths straight.
Proverbs 3:5-6

APPLICATION

Through the power of prayer the wounded can be healed, souls can be saved, lives can be protected, nations can be revived, and the world can be changed.

ADDITIONAL SCRIPTURES

John 15:7; Acts 12:5-19; 1 Timothy 2:1-5; James 5:13-18; 1 Peter 5:6-11

ILLUSTRATION

A missionary on furlough told this true story while visiting his home church in Michigan:

While serving at a small field hospital in Africa, every two weeks I traveled by bicycle through the jungle to a nearby city for supplies. This was a journey of two days and required camping overnight at the halfway point. On one of these journeys, I arrived in the city where I planned to collect money from a bank, purchase medicine and supplies, and then begin my two-day journey back to the field hospital. Upon arrival in the city, I observed two men fighting; one had been seriously injured. I treated him for his injuries and at the

same time witnessed to him about the Lord Jesus Christ. I then traveled two days, camping overnight and arrived home without incident.

Two weeks later I repeated my journey. Upon arriving in the city, I was approached by the young man I had treated. He told me that he had known I carried money and medicines. He said, "Some friends and I followed you into the jungle, knowing you would camp overnight. We planned to kill you and take your money and drugs. But just as we were about to move into your camp, we saw that you were surrounded by 26 armed guards."

At this I laughed and said that I was certainly all alone out at that jungle campsite. The young man pressed the point, however, and said, "No sir, I was not the only person to see the guards. My five friends also saw them, and we all counted them. It was because of those guards that we were afraid and left you alone."

At this point in the sermon, one of the men in the congregation jumped to his feet and interrupted the missionary and asked if he could tell him the exact day that this happened. The missionary told the congregation the date and the man who had interrupted told him this story:

> On the night of your incident in Africa, it was morning here and I was preparing to go play golf. I was about to putt the ball when I felt the urge to pray for you. In fact, the urging of the Lord was so strong, I left the green and called several men in the church to meet with me here in the sanctuary to pray for you. Would all of those men who met with me on that day stand up?

The men stood up. The missionary wasn't concerned with who they were; he was too busy counting how many men he saw. There were 26.

Pushing Against the Rock

KEY VERSE

Therefore, dear friends, since you already know this, be on your guard so that you may not be carried away by the error of lawless men and fall from your secure position. But grow in the grace and knowledge of our Lord and Savior Jesus Christ.
2 Peter 3:17-18

APPLICATION

Stick to what you feel is God's will and direction for your life. Do not be led away by the discouragement you may sometimes feel or the temptations that may distract you.

ADDITIONAL SCRIPTURES

Matthew 13:1-23; 24:45-51; John 14:15; Ephesians 4:11-16

ILLUSTRATION

There was a man who was asleep one night in his cabin when suddenly his room filled with light and the Savior appeared. The Lord told the man He had a task for him to do and showed him a large rock in front of his cabin. The Lord explained that the man was to push against the rock with all his might. This the man did, day after day.

For many years, the man toiled from sun up to sun down, his shoulders set squarely against the cold, massive surface of the unmoving rock, pushing with all his might. Each night the man returned to his cabin sore and worn out, feeling that his whole day had been spent in vain.

Seeing that the man was showing signs of discouragement, Satan decided to enter the picture, taunting the man. "You have been pushing against that rock for a long time and it hasn't budged," Satan whispered to the man. "Why kill yourself over this? You are never going to move it!"

These taunts discouraged and disheartened the man even more. *Why kill myself over this?* he thought. *From now on, I will put in my time, giving just the minimum of effort and that will be good enough.*

One day the man decided to take his troubled thoughts to the Lord. "Lord," he said, "I have labored long and hard in Your service, putting all my strength to do that which You have asked. Yet, after all this time, I have not even budged that rock the tiniest bit. What is wrong? Why am I failing?"

To this the Lord responded compassionately, "My friend, when long ago I asked you to serve Me and you accepted, I told you that your task was to push against the rock with all your strength, which you have done. Never once did I mention to you that I expected you to move it. Your task was to push. And now you come to Me, your strength spent, thinking that you have failed. But is that really so? Look at yourself. Your arms are strong and muscled, your back is brown, your hands are calloused from constant pressure and your legs have become massive and hard. Through opposition you have grown much and your abilities now surpass those which you used to have. No, you haven't moved the rock—but your calling was to be obedient, to push and to exercise your faith and trust in My wisdom. This you have done. And now I, My friend, will move the rock."

Remembering to Forget

KEY VERSE

Get rid of all bitterness, rage and anger, brawling and slander, along with every form of malice. Be kind and compassionate to one another, forgiving each other, just as in Christ God forgave you.
Ephesians 4:31-32

APPLICATION

Don't let grudges and bitterness cloud your days. Forgive and move on as God would do for you. Bright days will come your way—maybe they'll even come the way of those you have forgiven.

ADDITIONAL SCRIPTURES

Matthew 5:43-48; 18:21-35; Titus 3:1-3

ILLUSTRATION

Clara Barton, the founder of the American Red Cross, understood the importance of choosing a right attitude even in wrong situations. She was never known to hold a grudge against anyone. One time a friend recalled to her a cruel thing that had happened to her some years previously, but Clara seemed not to remember the incident. "Don't you remember the wrong that was done to you?" the friend asked.

"No," Clara answered calmly. "I distinctly remember forgetting that."

The Royal Robe

KEY VERSE

Therefore, since we are surrounded by such a great cloud of witnesses, let us throw off everything that hinders and the sin that so easily entangles, and let us run with perseverance the race marked out for us. Let us fix our eyes on Jesus, the author and perfecter of our faith, who for the joy set before him endured the cross, scorning its shame, and sat down at the right hand of the throne of God.
Hebrews 12:1-2

APPLICATION

How foolish we are never to fully accept the gift of salvation God offers to us, or to accept His gift but never fully enjoy it because we never let go of this world and our old things.

ADDITIONAL SCRIPTURES

Psalm 72:12-14; Proverbs 8:35-36; Luke 12:22-34; John 10:7-11

ILLUSTRATION

In a kingdom far away there once lived a beggar. He had been raised a beggar; his parents were beggars, as were their parents before them.

One day, as he was sitting at the gates of the kingdom, the beggar noticed one of the king's guards coming down the road. As the guard got closer, the beggar got a little nervous, so he hid in the shadows and continued to watch the guard. As the guard approached the gates, he got off his horse and hung a parchment on the wall.

Illustrations and Stories

When the guard left, the beggar came out of the shadows to read the sign. It was an invitation to a royal feast honoring the citizens of the kingdom. There were to be delicacies of all kinds and music and laughter, and both the king and prince would be there to celebrate with those who attended. The only condition for attending was that each person must wear a royal robe.

The beggar desperately wanted to attend the celebration, but he didn't have a royal robe. All he had was a bunch of old dirty, smelly rags. He would never be let into the banquet wearing these old things. Then it occurred to him. *Maybe I can go to the king and ask him if I could borrow a robe for the banquet*, he thought. *It doesn't even have to be a nice one. I'm sure he has many robes that he doesn't even wear anymore. I could ask him just to borrow it for the day and then return it.* This seemed like a pretty good idea, so off the beggar headed toward the castle.

As he drew nearer to the castle, the beggar began to wonder if his idea was really a good one. He might upset the king and be thrown in jail. *Still*, he thought, *what do I have to lose? I just want a chance to dine with the king and his prince.* So the beggar continued on. He came to the palace and inquired of the guard if he might have an audience with the king.

When the guard left, the beggar began to doubt himself again. He was about to leave when the guard returned and told the beggar to follow him into the palace. He was led into the very court of the king and stood before the king himself. The king asked the man what he desired, and the beggar explained to the king how he longed to be at the banquet but didn't have a robe to wear. At this, the king whispered into the ear of a guard who hurried out of the room.

When the guard returned, he was followed by the prince. The beggar thought this was the end; he had angered the king and now he would be imprisoned. The king whispered into the ear of the prince. The prince turned to the beggar and asked him to follow him into the next room. The beggar was very nervous now. Where was he being taken? The prince led the beggar into a room covered with mirrors. The prince approached one of the mirrors and pushed it open revealing a closet filled with robes. The beggar was overjoyed. The prince looked through all his robes and finally came to one. What he pulled out astonished the beggar. It was the most beautiful robe he had ever seen, even more beautiful than the prince's or king's royal robes.

As the beggar protested that the robe was much too beautiful for him to wear, the prince insisted. Finally, reluctantly the beggar accepted the robe. Then the prince explained, "This is a special robe. You will never need another garment as long as you wear it. It will never wear out, tear or get dirty. You no longer have need of those rags you now wear. This is the last garment you will ever need."

The beggar took off his old rags and put on the robe. It was so light he barely felt its weight. He looked in the mirrors and it was as if he had been transformed by the robe. He looked less like a beggar and more like a prince. The prince then told the beggar to keep the robe. Once again, the beggar protested, but the prince insisted and told the beggar he would see him at the banquet. As he left the room, the beggar spotted his old rags in the corner. He thought, *What if the prince is wrong? What if the robe does get torn or I do get it dirty? I'd better keep my old rags in case I need them.*

The banquet came and all the guests assembled. The feast was enormous and there was more food than the beggar had seen in his entire life. He sat at the table and placed his rags on his lap. As the food was passed down the table and as each guest had his fill of the delicacies, the beggar would oftentimes miss some, as he was always fidgeting with his rags. They would fall onto the floor and as he bent to pick them up some wonderful pastry would pass by. Still, he ate his fill and left the banquet satisfied.

The beggar lived out the rest of his life continuing to beg and continuing to carry his rags around. All the people of the city knew him, but interestingly, no one ever noticed his beautiful robe. The people only wondered why he always carried those dirty old rags around.

Finally, as the beggar was dying, news got back to the prince who was now king. He desired to bring cheer to the beggar in his last days. He found the beggar in an old shack in the city and entered into it. As the king entered the dying man's room, his joy left him and he was greatly saddened, for there, at the old beggar's side, was his pile of rags. As he saw the king's expression change, the beggar knew what he had done; he had wasted a life of royalty by carrying around his old rags.

Say a Prayer

KEY VERSE

Is any one of you in trouble? He should pray. Is anyone happy? Let him sing songs of praise. Is any one of you sick? He should call the elders of the church and to pray over him and anoint him with oil in the name of the Lord. And the prayer offered in faith will make the sick person well; the Lord will raise him up. If he has sinned, he will be forgiven.
James 5:13-15

APPLICATION

Pray for those around you in need. God really does listen and He will answer the prayers of the righteous.

ADDITIONAL SCRIPTURES

Numbers 12:10-16; Mark 11:23-24; Acts 9:36-43; 1 Timothy 2:1-3

ILLUSTRATION

I was taking my usual morning walk when a garbage truck pulled up beside me. I thought the driver was going to ask for directions. Instead, he showed me a picture of a cute little five-year-old boy. "This is my grandson, Jeremiah," he said. "He's on a life-support system at a Phoenix hospital."

Thinking he would next ask for a contribution to his hospital bills, I reached for my wallet. But he wanted something more valuable than money. He said, "I'm asking everybody I can to say a prayer for him. Would you say one for him, please?"

I did. And my problems didn't seem like much that day.

Spend Time Wisely

KEY VERSE

Be very careful, then, how you live—not as unwise but as wise, making the most of every opportunity, because the days are evil.
Ephesians 5:15-16

APPLICATION

God gives us each day as a gift. Investing our time wisely is an act of good stewardship.

ADDITIONAL SCRIPTURES

Romans 14:12; 1 Corinthians 4:2; Colossians 4:5

ILLUSTRATION

Imagine there is a financial institution that deposits $86,400 to your account each morning, carries over no balance from one day to the next and every evening cancels whatever part of the amount you had failed to use during the day. What would you do? Draw out every cent, of course! Well, everyone has such a bank. Its name is Time.

Every morning Time credits you with 86,400 seconds. Every night it writes off as lost whatever you have failed to invest to good purpose. It carries over no balance. It allows no overdraft. Each morning it opens a new account for you. Each night it burns the records of the day. If you fail to use the day's deposits, the loss is yours. There is no going back. There is no drawing against tomorrow.

You must live in the present on today's deposits. Invest it so as to get from it the utmost in health, happiness and success. The clock is running!

- Make the most of today.
- Treasure every moment that you have.
- Time and life are precious; learn to live above and beyond the line and you'll never have to live to regret the things you didn't do!

Standing Firm in Faith

KEY VERSE

*Be faithful, even to the point of death,
and I will give you the crown of life.*
Revelation 2:10

APPLICATION

The depth of your faith is revealed in trying circumstances. The person with vital faith will stand firm in the midst of trials and will receive God's rewards.

ADDITIONAL SCRIPTURES

Mark 8:35; Luke 9:26; 2 Corinthians 2:15; Philippians 1:27-28

ILLUSTRATION

Richard Wombrandt was a pastor in Moscow during the rise of Communism in Russia when the government called a meeting of pastors. All the pastors and their wives gathered, waiting in a room for the meeting to start.

Finally, a large group of armed soldiers and Communist leaders came into the room. The main Communist leader stood in front of the line of soldiers and announced, "Pastors, Communism is the same as Christianity." He then said, "You will all repeat that with me."

The armed soldiers moved in closer and all of the pastors repeated it—except Wombrandt. The main Communist leader repeated himself louder this time. "Communism is the same as Christianity."

The rest of the pastors repeated the phrase even louder, but Wombrandt just sat there, silent.

Wombrandt's wife said to him, "Stand up and do something about this."

He replied, "But I might never see you again."

Her response was wise and courageous, "I would rather not have a husband than a husband who is ashamed of Christ."

Bravely, Wombrandt stood up and said, "No! Communism is not the same as Christianity."

Because he stood up for what he believed, Wombrandt went to jail for seven years—time he would later refer to as the most glorious years of his life.

That is taking a stand. That is real, unwavering Christianity.

Staying Connected

KEY VERSE

Two are better than one, because they have a good return for their work: If one falls down, his friend can help him up. But pity the man who falls and has no one to help him up! Also, if two lie down together, they will keep warm. But how can one keep warm alone? Though one may be overpowered, two can defend themselves. A cord of three strands is not quickly broken.
Ecclesiastes 4:9-12

APPLICATION

Working with others will help get a project done faster and easier—and can make it a lot more fun.

ADDITIONAL SCRIPTURES

Exodus 17:8-16; Ruth 1:16-18; Proverbs 17:17; 27:10; John 15:12-17

ILLUSTRATION

As the pioneers moved west, each was given 40 acres of land. At first, they built their houses in the middle of their plots. But later, as more settlers moved in, they built on one of the four corners closest to their neighbors. The pioneers learned through experience that fellowship and community were more important than space and isolation.

Telemachus

KEY VERSE

For to me, to live is Christ and to die is gain.
Philippians 1:21

APPLICATION

Standing up for your faith may have tremendous effects.

ADDITIONAL SCRIPTURES

Matthew 10:16-18; 28:18-20; John 15:18-25; 1 Peter 2:20-22

ILLUSTRATION

In the fourth century there lived an Asian monk who spent most of his life in a remote community of prayer, raising vegetables for the cloister kitchen. When he was not tending his garden spot, he was fulfilling his vocation of study and prayer.

Then one day this monk named Telemachus felt that the Lord wanted him to go to Rome, the capital of the world. Telemachus had no idea why he should go there, and he was terrified at the thought. But as he prayed, God's directive became clear.

How bewildered the little monk must have been as he set out on the long journey on foot over the dusty roads westward, with everything he owned on his back. Why was he going? He didn't know. What would he find there? He had no idea. But obediently, he went.

Telemachus arrived in Rome during the holiday festival. You may know that the Roman rulers kept the ghettos quiet in those days by providing free bread and special entertainment called circuses. At the time Telemachus

arrived, the city was bustling with excitement over the recent Roman victory over the Goths. In the midst of this jubilant commotion, the monk looked for clues as to why God had brought him there, for he had no other guidance, not even a superior in a religious order to contact.

Perhaps, he thought, *it is not sheer coincidence that I have arrived at the festival time. Perhaps God has some special role for me to play.*

So Telemachus let the crowds guide him, and the stream of humanity soon led him into the Colosseum where the gladiator contests were to be staged. He could hear the cries of the animals in their cages beneath the floor of the great arena and the clamor of the contestants preparing to do battle.

The gladiators marched into the arena, saluted the emperor and shouted, "We who are about to die salute thee." Telemachus shuddered. He had never heard of the gladiator games before, but he had a premonition of awful violence.

The crowd had come to cheer men who, for no reason other than amusement, would murder each other. Human lives were offered for entertainment. As the monk realized what was going to happen, he realized that he could not sit still and watch such savagery. Neither could he leave and forget. He jumped to the top of the perimeter wall and cried, "In the name of Christ, forbear!"

The fighting began, of course. No one paid the slightest heed to the puny voice. So Telemachus pattered down the stone steps and leapt onto the sandy floor of the arena. He made a comic figure—a scrawny man in a monk's habit dashing back and forth between muscular armed athletes. One gladiator sent him sprawling with a blow from his shield, directing him back to his seat. It was a rough gesture, though almost a kind one. The crowd roared.

But Telemachus refused to stop. He rushed into the way of those trying to fight, shouting again, "In the name of Christ, forbear!" The crowd began to laugh and cheer him on, perhaps thinking him part of the entertainment.

Then his movement blocked the vision of one of the contestants and the gladiator saw the blow coming just in time. Furious now, the crowd began to cry for the interloper's blood.

"Run him through," they screamed.

The gladiator he had blocked raised his sword and with a flash of steel struck Telemachus, slashing down across his chest and into his stomach. The little monk gasped once more, "In the name of Christ, forbear."

Then a strange thing occurred. As the two gladiators and the crowd focused on the still form on the suddenly crimson sand, the arena grew deathly quiet. In the silence, someone on the top tier got up and walked out. Another followed. All over the arena, spectators began to leave, until the huge stadium was emptied.

There were other forces at work, of course, but that innocent figure lying in a pool of blood crystallized the opposition, and that was the last gladiatorial contest in the Roman Colosseum. Never again did men kill each other for the crowd's entertainment in the Roman arena.

—Charles Colson,
Loving God
(Grand Rapids, MI:
Zondervan, 1983),
pp. 241-243.

The Test

KEY VERSE

> *The LORD does not look at the things man looks at. Man looks at the outward appearance, but the LORD looks at the heart.*
> 1 Samuel 16:7

APPLICATION

Where do we see the beauty in people? So often it is only through their outward appearance, but true beauty is seen in the heart, mind and soul of a godly person.

ADDITIONAL SCRIPTURES

Proverbs 31:30; Isaiah 53:2; Romans 10:15; 1 Peter 3:3-5

ILLUSTRATION

John Blanchard stood up from the bench, straightened his Army uniform and studied the crowd of people making their way through Grand Central Station. He looked for the girl whose heart he knew but whose face he didn't—the girl with the rose. His interest in her began 13 months before in a Florida library.

Taking a book off the shelf, he found himself intrigued, not with the words of the book, but with the notes penciled in the margin. The soft handwriting reflected a thoughtful soul and insightful mind. In the front of the book, he discovered the previous owner's name, Miss Hollis Maynell. With time and effort he located her address. She lived in New York City. He wrote her a letter introducing himself and inviting her to correspond. The next day he was shipped overseas for service in World War II.

During the next year and one month, the two grew to know each other through the mail. Each letter was a seed falling on a fertile heart. A romance was budding. Blanchard requested a photograph, but she refused. She felt that if he really cared, it wouldn't matter what she looked like. When the day finally came for him to return from Europe, they scheduled their first meeting. It was to be at 7:00 P.M. in Grand Central Station in New York.

"You'll recognize me," she wrote, "by the red rose I'll be wearing on my lapel."

At 7:00 P.M., John Blanchard was in the station looking for a girl whose heart he loved but whose face he'd never seen. Mr. Blanchard tells what happened next:

A young woman was coming toward me, her figure long and slim. Her blonde hair lay back in curls from her delicate ears; her eyes were blue as flowers. Her lips and chin had a gentle firmness, and in her pale green suit, she was like springtime come alive. I started toward her, entirely forgetting to notice that she was not wearing a rose. As I moved, a small, provocative smile curved her lips.

"Going my way, sailor?" she murmured.

Almost uncontrollably I made one step closer to her, and then I saw Hollis Maynell. She was standing almost directly behind the girl. A woman well past 40, she had graying hair tucked under a worn hat. She was more than plump, her thick-ankled feet thrust into low-heeled shoes.

The girl in the green suit was walking quickly away. I felt as though I was split in two, so keen was my desire to follow her and yet so deep was my longing for the woman whose spirit had truly companioned me and upheld my own. And there she stood.

Her pale, plump face was gentle and sensible; her gray eyes had a warm and kindly twinkle. I did not hesitate. My fingers gripped the small worn blue leather copy of the book that was to identify me to her. This would not be love, but it would be something precious, something perhaps even better than love, a friendship for which I had been and must ever be grateful.

I squared my shoulders and saluted and held out the book to the woman, even though while I spoke I felt choked by the bitterness of my disappointment.

"I'm Lieutenant John Blanchard, and you must be Miss Maynell. I am so glad you could meet me; may I take you to dinner?" The woman's face broadened into a tolerant smile.

"I don't know what this is about, son," she answered, "but the young lady in the green suit who just went by begged me to wear this rose on my coat. And she said if you were to ask me out to dinner, I should tell you that she is waiting for you in the big restaurant across the street. She said it was some kind of test!"

It's not difficult to understand and admire Miss Maynell's wisdom. The true nature of a heart is seen in its response to the unattractive. "Tell me whom you love," Houssaye wrote, "and I will tell you who you are."

Contributed by
Mikey's Funnies
Youth Specialties

Those with the Least Sometimes Give the Most

KEY VERSE

As he looked up, Jesus saw the rich putting their gifts into the temple treasury. He also saw a poor widow put in two very small copper coins. "I tell you the truth," he said, "this poor widow has put in more than all the others. All these people gave their gifts out of their wealth; but she out of her poverty put in all she had to live on."
Luke 21:1-4

APPLICATION

At times, poor people demonstrate greater generosity than rich people. When people give out of their poverty, they become rich in faith—which is more valuable than any worldly wealth.

ADDITIONAL SCRIPTURES

Acts 20:35; 2 Corinthians 6:10; 8:1-15; 9:6-15; 1 Timothy 6:18-19; James 2:5

ILLUSTRATION

I'll never forget Easter, 1946. I was 14, my little sister Lucy was 12, and my older sister Darlene was 16. We lived at home with our mother, and the four of us knew what it was to do without many things. My dad had died five years before, leaving Mom with seven young children to raise and no money.

By 1946 my older sisters were married and my brothers

had left home. A month before Easter, the pastor of our church announced that a special Easter offering would be taken to help a poor family. He asked everyone to save and give sacrificially.

When we got home, we talked about what we could do. We decided to buy 50 pounds of potatoes and live on them for a month. This would allow us to save $20 of our grocery money for the offering. If we kept our lights turned out as much as possible and didn't listen to the radio, we'd save money on that month's electric bill. Darlene got as many house- and yard-cleaning jobs as possible, and both of us baby-sat for everyone we could. For 15¢ we could buy enough cotton loops to make a set of three potholders which we could sell for $1.

That month was one of the best of our lives. Every day we counted the money to see how much we had saved. We had even made $20 on the potholders! At night we'd sit in the dark and talk about how the poor family was going to enjoy having the money the church would give them. We had about 80 people in church, so we figured that whatever amount of money we had to give, the offering would surely be 20 times that much. After all, every Sunday the pastor had reminded everyone to save for the sacrificial offering.

The day before Easter, Lucy and I walked to the grocery store and got the manager to give us three crisp $20 bills and one $10 bill in exchange for our many coins and smaller bills.

We ran all the way home to show Mom and Darlene. We had never had so much money before.

That night we were so excited we could hardly sleep. We didn't care that we wouldn't have new clothes for Easter; we had $70 for the sacrificial offering.

We could hardly wait to get to church! On Sunday morning, rain was pouring. We didn't own an umbrella, and the church was over a mile from our home, but it didn't seem to matter how wet we got. Darlene had cardboard in her shoes to fill the holes. The cardboard came apart and her feet got wet, but we sat in church proudly. I heard some teenagers talking about the "Smith girls wearing their old dresses." I looked at them in their new clothes, and I felt rich.

When the sacrificial offering was taken, we were sitting in the second row from the front. Mom put in the $10 bill, and each of us kids put in a $20 bill.

As we walked home after church, we sang all the way.

At lunch Mom had a surprise for us. She had bought a dozen eggs, and we had boiled Easter eggs with our fried potatoes! Late that afternoon the minister drove up in his car. Mom went to the door, talked with him for a moment and then came back with an envelope in her hand. We asked what it was, but she didn't say a word. She opened the envelope and out fell a bunch of money. There were three crisp $20 bills, one $10 and seventeen $1 bills.

Mom put the money back in the envelope. We didn't talk, just sat and stared at the floor. We had gone from feeling like millionaires to feeling like poor white trash. We kids had such a happy life that we felt sorry for anyone who didn't have our mom and dad for parents and a house full of siblings and other kids visiting constantly. We thought it was fun to share silverware and see whether we got the spoon or the fork each night. We had two knives that we passed around to whoever needed them.

I knew we didn't have a lot of things that other people had, but I'd never thought we were poor. That Easter day I found out we were. The minister had brought us the money for the poor family, so we must be poor. I didn't like being poor. I looked at my dress and worn-out shoes and felt so ashamed that I didn't even want to go back to church. Everyone there probably already knew we were poor!

I thought about school. I was in the ninth grade and at the top of my class of over 100 students. I wondered if the kids at school knew that we were poor. I decided that I could quit school since I had finished the eighth grade. That was all the law required at that time. We sat in silence for a long time. Then it got dark and we went to bed. All that week, we girls went to school and came home, and no one talked much. Finally on Saturday, Mom asked us what we wanted to do with the money. What did poor people do with money? We didn't know. We'd never known we were poor. We didn't want to go to church on Sunday, but Mom said we had to. Although it was a sunny day, we didn't talk on the way. Mom started to sing, but no one joined in and so she only sang one verse.

At church we had a missionary speaker. He talked about how churches in Africa made buildings out of sun-dried bricks, but they needed money to buy roofs. He said that $100 would put a roof on a church. The minister said, "Can't we all sacrifice to help these poor people?" We looked at each other and smiled for the first time in a week.

Mom reached into her purse and pulled out the envelope. She passed it to Darlene. Darlene gave it to me, and I handed it to Lucy, who placed it in the offering.

When the offering was counted, the minister announced that it was "a little over $100." The missionary was excited. He hadn't expected such a large offering from our small church. He said, "You must have some rich people in this church." Suddenly it struck us! We had given $87 of that "little over $100."

We were the *rich* family in the church! Hadn't the missionary said so? From that day on I've never been poor again. I've always remembered how rich I am—because I have Jesus!

True Beauty

KEY VERSE

The Lord does not look at the things man looks at. Man looks at the outward appearance, but the Lord looks at the heart.
1 Samuel 16:7

APPLICATION

Outer beauty is fragile and fades. Inner beauty is what matters. Jesus demonstrated that outer scars often reflect loving sacrifice.

ADDITIONAL SCRIPTURES

Proverbs 20:30; 31:30; Isaiah 53:1-3; John 20:24-28; Galatians 6:17; Ephesians 3:13; Hebrews 12:3-4; 1 Peter 3:4-5

ILLUSTRATION

A little boy brought home an invitation from his elementary school, inviting his mother to attend a parent-teacher conference. To the little boy's dismay, the mother announced she intended to go.

This would be the first time that the little boy's classmates and teacher would meet his mother and he was embarrassed by her appearance. Although she was a beautiful woman, there was a severe scar that covered nearly all of the right side of her face. The boy had never asked how she got the scar; he only knew that it was ugly.

At the conference, students and teachers alike were impressed by the kindness and natural beauty of his mother. No one seemed to be as disgusted by the mother's scar

as her son was. The little boy, embarrassed, hid himself from everyone. He did, however, get within earshot of a conversation between his mother and his teacher.

"How did you get the scar on your face?" the teacher asked.

The mother replied, "When my son was a baby, he was in a room that caught fire. I ran in, but as I entered the room, I saw a beam coming down from the ceiling and I placed myself over his crib trying to shield him. I was knocked unconscious, but fortunately, a fireman came in and saved the both of us."

She touched the burned side of her face. "This scar will be permanent, but to this day, I have never regretted doing what I did."

At this point the little boy with tears in his eyes came running toward his mother. He hugged her and felt an overwhelming sense of the sacrifice that his mother had made for him. He held her hand tightly—and proudly—for the rest of the day.

The True Meaning of the Candy Cane

KEY VERSE

For the message of the cross is foolishness to those who are perishing, but to us who are being saved it is the power of God.
1 Corinthians 1:18

APPLICATION

The true meaning of Christmas is the good news of a pure and holy God becoming a man and enduring the cross for all of us. We must share that good news with others.

ADDITIONAL SCRIPTURES

Matthew 1:22-23; Mark 4:23; 1 Corinthians 1:22-25; Philippians 2:5-11; 2 Timothy 4:1-5; Hebrews 12:2-3

ILLUSTRATION

Many years ago as the Christmas season approached, a humble candymaker living in a small town in the state of Indiana wanted to create something with his hands that would be symbolic of the true meaning of Christmas. Although his creation has become known throughout the world simply as a candy cane, it actually offers an often needed reminder of the birth, ministry and death of Jesus Christ! This is that story as told through a simple piece of candy:

As a believer, the candymaker began with pure, hard, white candy—white to symbolize the virgin

birth and the sinless nature of Jesus and hard to represent Christ as the solid rock, the foundation of the Church and the firmness of the promises of God.

The candymaker then shaped the candy into the form of a *J* representing both the precious name of Jesus and also His staff as the Good Shepherd who reaches down into the ditches of the world to lift out His fallen lambs, bringing them into eternal salvation.

The candymaker then stained the candy with red stripes to represent the scourging Jesus received and the blood He shed on the cross as redemption for each who will believe in Him and accept Him as Lord.

His final act was to make his creation and all that it stood for available to everyone—to partake and to experience its sweetness. Thus, the candy-maker hung the candy abundantly on the Christmas tree in his shop, around the window and the door frame, offering it for free to anyone who would enter the shop and ask.

Unfortunately, as with many other things now associated with the commercialism of Christmas, the candy cane has become to most of the world just an inexpensive decoration for trees and fireplaces. But like a parable, for those who have ears to hear (see Mark 4:23) it's real message is the birth, life and ministry of Christ Jesus for whom this holiday is celebrated.

From this day forward, may every candy cane you see remind you of this story. May it also provide you with the opportunity to use this little piece of sweetness to share with at least one friend, relative, classmate or coworker the true meaning of Christmas and the good news of Jesus Christ!

Trust and Obey

KEY VERSE

Trust in the LORD with all your heart and lean not on your own understanding; in all your ways acknowledge him, and he will make your paths straight.
Proverbs 3:5-6

APPLICATION

The safest place for us to be is wherever we are when we trust and obey God. He knows what is best for us, even when we don't understand.

ADDITIONAL SCRIPTURES

Leviticus 25:18; 1 Samuel 15:22; Proverbs 29:25; Jeremiah 17:7; Nahum 1:7; Luke 11:28; Romans 8:28

ILLUSTRATION

A missionary and his son went for a walk in the jungles of Africa. It was their routine to do so every morning. The boy was very young and did everything that his father told him to. One day, the boy went ahead of his father and was playing in the grass near some trees when suddenly the father shouted for his son. He yelled his name and directed him to lie down. Not understanding but totally trusting his father, he obeyed. The father then directed him to crawl out of the grass. Still not understanding why, he crawled toward his father.

When the boy reached his father, he was greeted with a huge hug. His father praised his obedience and told him what a good boy he was for doing as he had been directed. Even though he did not understand why, he had done what his father had asked. The father then turned the boy around to show him why he was told to do all of these things. Above the area where he had been playing was a huge boa constrictor that would have squeezed the life out of him had he remained standing where he had been.

Two Nickels and Five Pennies

KEY VERSE

> *But God chose the foolish things of the world to shame the wise; God chose the weak things of the world to shame the strong.*
> 1 Corinthians 1:27

APPLICATION

Do not judge on first glance because there maybe something of value and significance just under the surface—and it may be a blessing from God.

ADDITIONAL SCRIPTURES

Matthew 11:25; Romans 2:1-2; James 2:1-13

ILLUSTRATION

When ice cream sundaes cost much less, a boy entered a coffee shop and sat at the table. A waitress put a glass of water in front of him. "How much is an ice cream sundae?"

"Fifty cents," replied the waitress.

The little boy pulled his hand out of his pocket and studied a number of coins in it. "How much is a dish of plain ice cream?" he inquired.

Some people were now waiting for a table, and the waitress was impatient. "Thirty-five cents," she said angrily.

The little boy again counted the coins. "I'll have the plain ice cream."

The waitress brought the ice cream and walked away. The boy finished, paid the cashier and departed. When the waitress came back, she swallowed hard at what she saw. There, placed neatly beside the empty dish, were two nickels and five pennies—her tip.

The Value of Knowing Jesus

KEY VERSE

Whatever was to my profit I now consider loss for the sake of Christ. What is more, I consider everything a loss compared to the surpassing greatness of knowing Christ Jesus my Lord, for whose sake I have lost all things. I consider them rubbish, that I may gain Christ.
Philippians 3:7-8

APPLICATION

Having a personal relationship with Jesus brings with it the most valuable possession you can ever have: eternal life!

ADDITIONAL SCRIPTURES

Matthew 13:44-46; John 5:24; 17:3; Romans 8:17; Ephesians 1:14; 1 Peter 1:4

ILLUSTRATION

A wealthy man and his son loved to collect rare works of art. They had everything in their collection, from Raphael to Picasso. They would often sit together and admire the great works they had collected.

When the Vietnam conflict broke out, the son went to war. He was very courageous and died in battle while rescuing another soldier. The father was notified, and he grieved deeply for his only son.

About a month later, just before Christmas, there was a knock at the door. A young man stood at the door with a large package in his hands. He said, "Sir, you don't know

me, but I am the soldier for whom your son gave his life. He saved many lives that day, and he was carrying me to safety when a bullet struck him in the heart and he died instantly. He often talked about you and your love for art."

The young man held out his package. "I know this isn't much," he continued. "I'm not really a great artist, but I think your son would have wanted you to have this."

The father opened the package. It was a portrait of his son painted by the young man. He stared in awe at the way the soldier had captured the personality of his son in the painting. The father was so drawn to the painting that his eyes welled up with tears. He thanked the young man and offered to pay him for the picture. "Oh no, sir, I could never repay what your son did for me. It's a gift."

The father hung the portrait over his mantle. Every time visitors came to his home, he took them to see the portrait of his son before he showed them any of the other great works he had collected.

The man died a few months later. There was to be a great auction of his paintings. Many influential people gathered, excited about seeing the great paintings and having an opportunity to purchase one for their collection.

On the platform sat the painting of the son. The auctioneer pounded his gavel. "We will start the bidding with this picture of the son. Who will bid for this picture?"

There was silence. Then a voice in the back of the room shouted, "We want to see the famous paintings. Skip this one!"

But the auctioneer persisted. "Will someone bid for this painting? Who will start the bidding? $100? $200?"

Another voice shouted angrily, "We didn't come to see this painting. We came to see the Van Goghs, the Rembrandts. Get on with the real art!"

But still the auctioneer continued, "The son! The son! Who'll take the son?"

Finally, a voice came from the very back of the room. "I'll give $10 for the painting." It was the longtime gardener of the man and his son. Being a poor man, he could afford to offer only $10.

"We have $10. Who will bid $20?"

"Give it to him for $10. Let's see the masters."

"$10 is the bid. Won't someone bid $20?"

The crowd was becoming angry. They weren't interested in the picture of the son. They wanted the more worthy investments for their collections.

The auctioneer pounded the gavel. "Going once, twice, SOLD for $10!"

A man sitting on the second row shouted, "Now let's get on with the collection!"

The auctioneer laid down his gavel and said, "I'm sorry, the auction is over."

"What about the paintings?" someone asked.

"I am sorry. When I was called to conduct this auction, I was told of a secret stipulation in the will. I was not allowed to reveal that stipulation until this time. Only the painting of the son would be auctioned. Whoever bought that painting would inherit the entire estate, including the other paintings. The man who took the portrait of the son gets everything!"

God gave His Son over 2,000 years ago to die for our sins on a cruel cross. Much like the auctioneer, His message today is "The Son, the Son—who'll take the Son?" You see, whoever takes the Son gets everything.

What If . . .

KEY VERSE

This is love: not that we loved God, but that he loved us and sent his Son as an atoning sacrifice for our sins.
1 John 4:10

APPLICATION

Oh that we would comprehend God's great love and return it with such passion as to begin to embrace Him with the love He so deserves.

ADDITIONAL SCRIPTURES

Psalms 136; Romans 8:31-39; Ephesians 3:16-19; 1 John 4:7-9,11-19

ILLUSTRATION

What if God couldn't take the time to bless us today because we couldn't take the time to thank Him yesterday?

What if God decided to stop leading us tomorrow because we didn't follow Him today?

What if we never saw another flower bloom because we grumbled when God sent the rain?

What if God didn't walk with us today because we failed to recognize it as His day?

What if God took away the Bible tomorrow because we would not read it today?

What if God took away His message because we failed to listen to His messenger?

What if the door of the Church was closed because we did not open the door of our hearts?

Illustrations and Stories

What if God stopped loving and caring for us because we failed to love and care for others?

What if God would not hear us today because we would not listen to Him yesterday?

What if God answered our prayers the way we answer His call for service?

What if God met our needs the way we give Him our lives?

Funnies

Funnies

Albert Einstein and His Chauffeur

A story is told about Albert Einstein who, when he was making the rounds of the speaker's circuit, usually found himself eagerly longing to get back to his laboratory work. One night as they were driving to yet another rubber-chicken dinner, Einstein mentioned to his chauffeur (a man who somewhat resembled Einstein in looks and manner) that he was tired of speech making.

"I have an idea, boss," his chauffeur said. "I've heard you give this speech so many times, I'll bet I could give it for you."

Einstein laughed loudly and said, "Why not? Let's do it!"

When they arrived at the dinner, Einstein donned the chauffeur's cap and jacket and sat in the back of the room. The chauffeur gave a beautiful rendition of Einstein's speech and even expertly answered a few questions.

Then a supremely pompous professor asked an extremely esoteric question about antimatter formation, digressing here and there to let everyone in the audience know that he was nobody's fool.

Without missing a beat, the chauffeur fixed the professor with a steely stare and said, "Sir, the answer to that question is so simple that I will let my chauffeur, who is sitting in the back, answer it for me."

And You Thought You Had Problems

A man was working on his motorcycle on his backyard patio while his wife worked in the kitchen. The man was racing the engine and somehow the motorcycle slipped into gear. The motorcycle smashed through the patio door, dragging the surprised man, who was still holding the handlebars.

The wife ran into the dining room to find her husband lying on the floor, bleeding. She ran to the phone and summoned an ambulance, explaining that because they lived on a fairly large hill, she would go down the several flights of long steps to the street to direct the paramedics to her husband.

After the ambulance arrived and transported the husband to the hospital, the wife uprighted the motorcycle and pushed it outside. Seeing that gas had spilled on the floor, the wife got some paper towels, blotted up the gasoline and, not knowing what else to do with them, threw them into the toilet.

After arriving home later that evening, the husband looked at the shattered patio door and the damage done to his motorcycle. He became despondent and went into the bathroom, sat on the toilet and smoked a cigarette. After finishing the cigarette, he flipped it between his legs into the toilet bowl.

The wife heard a loud explosion and ran into the bathroom to find her husband lying on the floor, burned in the worst possible places. Once again, the wife ran to the phone and called for an ambulance. The paramedics loaded the husband on the stretcher and began carrying him to the street.

While they were going down the stairs to the street, one of the paramedics asked the wife how her husband had burned himself. When she answered, the paramedics carrying the man started laughing so hard, one of them tipped the stretcher and dumped the husband out. He fell down the remaining steps and broke his ankle.

Are You an Optimist or a Pessimist?

There is a story of identical twins. One was a hope-filled optimist. "Everything is coming up roses!" he would say. The other was a sad and hopeless pessimist; he thought that the author of Murphy's Law was an optimist. The worried parents of the boys brought them to the local psychologist.

He suggested to the parents a plan to balance the twins' personalities. "On their next birthday, put them in separate rooms to open their gifts. Give the pessimist the best toys you can afford, and give the optimist a box of manure." The parents followed these instructions and carefully observed the results.

When they peeked in on the pessimist, they heard him audibly complaining, "I don't like the color of this computer. I'll bet this calculator will break. I don't like this game. I know someone who's got a bigger toy car than this."

Tiptoeing across the corridor, the parents peeked in and saw their little optimist gleefully throwing his smelly gift in the air. He was giggling, "You can't fool me! Where there's this much manure there *must* be a pony for me somewhere!"

Carjacking Foiled

Upon returning from her shopping trip, an elderly lady walked to her car to find four young men in it. She dropped her shopping bags, drew her handgun from her purse and proceeded to scream at the top of her voice, "I know how to use this and I will if I have to! Get out of that car!"

The four men didn't wait around for a second invitation to exit the car—they got out and ran like mad, whereupon the lady proceeded to load her shopping bags into the back of the car. As she settled comfortably into the driver's seat and prepared to start the car, she discovered that her key didn't fit the ignition.

Feeling a bit silly, she realized that the car she was in wasn't her car at all! She got out and found her car just four spaces away, where she loaded her bags and immediately drove to the police station.

The sergeant to whom she told the story nearly fell apart with laughter and pointed to the other end of the counter—where four pale young men were reporting a carjacking by a mad elderly woman. No charges were filed.

A Church Split

After surviving 10 lonely years deserted on an island, a man is finally rescued. One of his rescuers notices three huts and asks, "What is the first hut for?"

"That's my home," the survivor replies.

"What is the second hut for?"

"That's my church."

"What is the third hut for?"

"Oh, that's the church I used to go to."

Didn't Want to Go to Church

A husband and his wife arose one Sunday morning and the wife dressed for church. It was just about time for the service when she noticed her husband hadn't moved a finger toward getting dressed.

Perplexed, the wife asked, "Why aren't you getting dressed for church?"

"Because I don't want to go," he replied.

"I see. Do you have any particular reason?"

"Yes, I have three good reasons. First, the congregation is cold. Second, no one likes me. And third, I just don't want to go."

The wife replied, wisely, "Well, Honey, I have three reasons why you should go. First, the congregation is warm. Second, there are a few people there who like you. And third, you're the pastor! So get dressed!"

Dinner Guests

A wife invited some people to dinner. At the table she asked her six-year-old daughter to say the blessing.

The girl replied, "I don't know what to say."

The mother told her, "Just say what you hear Mommy say."

The daughter bowed her head and said, "Lord, why on Earth did I invite all these people to dinner?"

The Elevator

An Amish boy and his father were visiting a mall. They were amazed by almost everything they saw but were especially intrigued by two shiny silver walls that could move apart and back together again.

The boy asked his father, "What is this, Father?" The father, having never seen an elevator before, responded, "Son, I have never seen anything like this in my life. I don't know what it is."

While the boy and his father were watching wide-eyed, an old lady with a cane slowly limped up to the moving walls and pressed a button. After a moment, the walls opened to reveal a small room. The lady walked into the room and the walls closed.

As the boy and his father watched, the numbers above the silver walls began to light up one by one. Then, the boy and his father watched as the numbers lit again, this time in reverse.

Suddenly, the silver walls opened again and out stepped a beautiful young woman.

Leaning over so as not to speak too loudly, the father said to his son, "Quick, my boy! Run and get your mother."

Funnies

Freefall

There were four people all on a small plane together. An hour into the plane ride the pilot announced that the plane was going down and that everyone would need to jump; then he put on his parachute and jumped—leaving only three parachutes for the four passengers.

The first passenger to grab a parachute was a doctor who explained that he was on the verge of discovering a cure for cancer; therefore, he was clearly the most important passenger. That said, he jumped out of the doomed plane.

The second passenger claimed to be the smartest man in the world. "Surely you wouldn't want the smartest man in the world to go down with the plane," he explained, and he jumped too.

The only two passengers left were a Boy Scout and a priest. The priest told the young boy that he had lived a good life and was ready to die, so the boy should take the parachute and jump to safety. The Boy Scout calmly answered, "Don't worry. There are still two parachutes left. 'The smartest man in the world' just jumped out of the plane with my knapsack."

God Will Provide

A nice girl brings her fiancé home to meet her parents. After dinner, her mother tells her father to find out about the young man.

The father invites the fiancé to his study for a chat. "So what are your plans?" the father asks.

"I'm a biblical scholar," the fiancé replies.

"A biblical scholar. Admirable, but what will you do to provide a nice house for my daughter to live in, as she's accustomed to?" the father asks.

"I will study and God will provide," comes the reply.

"And how will you buy her the beautiful engagement ring she deserves?"

"I will concentrate on my studies and God will provide."

"And children? How will you support children?"

"Don't worry, sir. God will provide."

The conversation proceeds, and each time the father's questions are answered with the fiancé insisting that God will provide.

Later that evening while getting ready for bed, the mother asks the father, "So how did it go?"

The father shrugs and says, "He has no plans for a future, no job prospects and he thinks I'm God."

God's Creation

One day a group of scientists got together and decided that man had come a long way and no longer needed God. So they picked one scientist to go and tell God that they didn't need Him anymore.

The chosen scientist walked up to God and said, "God, we've decided that we no longer need You. We're to the point that we can clone people and do many miraculous things, so why don't You just go on and get lost?"

God listened very patiently and kindly to the man. After the scientist was done talking, God said, "Very well, how about this? Let's have a man-making contest."

"OK, great!" the scientist replied.

God added, "Now, we're going to do this just like I did back in the old days with Adam."

The scientist said, quite sure of himself said, "Sure, no problem" and bent down to grab himself a handful of dirt.

God shook His finger at the scientist and said, "No, no, no. You'll have to get your *own* dirt!"

Only Opportunities

Barb and her husband, Chuck, a youth leader, had just arrived at the campground for a weekend retreat with their young peoples' group. While Chuck unloaded the van, Barb handed out room assignments. On the bulletin board of the lobby in the main lodge was a poster declaring, "There are no problems, only opportunities."

A boy named Jeff approached Barb and said, "Uh, Barb, I've got a problem."

Barb pointed to the sign and said, "Jeff, there are no problems, only opportunities."

"Well, if that's the way you want it," replied Jeff, "but there's a girl assigned to my room."

Payback

During the Korean War, some American soldiers rented a house and hired a local boy to do their housekeeping and cooking. It was common for soldiers to get that kind of setup for easy-come, easy-go, easy-pay. This particular Korean fellow had an unbelievably positive attitude and was always smiling.

To amuse themselves, the soldiers played one trick after another on the young man. They nailed his shoes to the floor, and he'd get up in the morning, pull the nails out with pliers and slip on his shoes, always maintaining his excellent spirit. They put grease on the stove handles, and he would wipe each one off, smiling and singing his way through the day. They balanced buckets of water over the door, and he'd get drenched, but he would dry off and never fuss, time after time.

Finally, the soldiers became so ashamed of themselves that they called the young man in one day and said, "We want you to know that we're never going to trick you again. Your attitude has been outstanding."

The young man asked, "You mean no more nail shoes to floor?"

"No more," came the reply.

"You mean no more sticky on stove knobs?"

"No more."

"You mean no more water buckets on door?"

"No more."

"OK then," the young man responded with a smile and a shrug. "No more spit in soup."

School Excuses

Here are some actual excuses received for students returning to school after an absence:

- My son is under a doctor's care and could not take PE yesterday. Please execute him.
- Please excuse Cynthia for being absent on Jan. 28, 29, 30, 31, 32, 33.
- Please excuse Danny for being. It was his father's fault.
- June could not come to school yesterday because she was bothered by very close veins.
- Richard had an acre in his side.
- Please excuse Timothy for being absent last week. He could not talk because of Larry and Gitus.
- Please excuse Nancy for staying home. The doctor said that her lungs are too full to be outside.
- Please excuse Margaret from Jim yesterday because she is administrating.
- Please excuse Robert for being absent. He had a cold and could not breed well.

Through the Eyes of a Child

Funnies

An old country doctor went way out to the boondocks to deliver a baby. It was so far out, there was no electricity. When the doctor arrived, no one was home except the laboring mother and her five-year-old child.

The doctor instructed the child to hold a lantern high, so he could see while he helped the woman deliver the baby. The mother pushed and after a little while, the doctor lifted the newborn baby by the feet and spanked him on the bottom to get him to take his first breath. The doctor then asked the five-year-old what he thought of the baby.

The young boy determinedly replied, "He shouldn't have crawled in there in the first place. Spank him again!"

Two Monks

Two monks on a pilgrimage came to the ford of a river, where they saw a girl dressed in all her finery. She obviously did not know what to do, since the river was high and she did not want to spoil her clothes. Without much ado, one of the monks took her on his back, carried her across and put her down on dry ground on the other side.

Then the monks continued on their way. After an hour the elder monk started complaining, "Surely it is not right to touch a woman; it is against the commandments to have close contact with a woman. How could you go against the rules of monks?"

The monk who had carried the girl walked along silently, but finally he remarked, "I sat the woman down by the river an hour ago. Why are *you* still carrying her?"

Value This Time in Your Life

Here's some valuable advice from the movie *City Slickers*:

Value this time in your life, kids, because this is the time in your life when you still have your choices. It goes by so fast.

When you're a teenager, you think you can do anything and you do. Your twenties are a blur.

Thirties you raise your family, you make a little money, and you think to yourself, *What happened to my twenties?*

Forties, you grow a little potbelly; you grow another chin. The music starts to get too loud; one of your old girlfriends from high school becomes a grandmother.

Fifties, you have a minor surgery—you'll call it a procedure, but it's a surgery.

Sixties, you'll have a major surgery, the music is still loud, but it doesn't matter because you can't hear it anyway.

Seventies, you and the wife retire to Fort Lauderdale. You start eating dinner at 2 o'clock in the afternoon, you have lunch around 10 o'clock, breakfast the night before, spend most of your time wandering around malls looking for the ultimate soft yogurt and muttering, "How come the kids don't call? How come the kids don't call?"

The eighties, you'll have a major stroke, and you end up babbling with some Jamaican nurse who your wife can't stand, but who you call "Mama."

Any questions?

Van Gogh's Family

After much careful research, it has been discovered that the famous artist Vincent Van Gogh had many relatives. Following are just a few:

- The obnoxious brother: Please Gogh
- The constipated uncle: Cant Gogh
- The prune-loving brother: Gotta Gogh
- The dizzy aunt: Verti Gogh
- The Illinois cousin: Chicag Gogh
- A positive-thinking aunt: Wayto Gogh
- The magician uncle: Wherediddy Gogh
- The disco-loving sister: Go Gogh
- The traveling niece: Winnebay Gogh
- The stagecoach-driving nephew: Wellsfar Gogh

Quotes

Attitude

Most people have a desire to look at the exception instead of the desire to become exceptional.

—John C. Maxwell, *Developing the Leader Within You*

* * * * *

I do not pray for a lighter load but for a stronger back.

—Phillips Brooks

* * * * *

Buried emotions are like buried waste; you can't ever truly get rid of them. They tend to fester and seep into other areas of our lives unless they are treated properly.

—Author unknown

* * * * *

People seldom notice old clothes if you wear a big smile.

—Lee Mildon

* * * * *

The only people with whom you should try to get even are those who have helped you.

—John E. Southard

* * * * *

The past is over, forget it. The future holds out hope, reach for it.

—Charles Swindoll

Quotes

You are only one thought away from a good feeling.

—Sheila Kristal

* * * * *

It is one thing to learn about the past; it is another to wallow in it.

—Kenneth Auchincloss

* * * * *

The great man is he who does not lose his child-heart.

—Mencius

* * * * *

One sees great things from the valley; only small things from the peak.

—G.K. Chesterton, *The Hammer of God*

* * * * *

The only disability in life is a bad attitude.

—Scott Hamilton

* * * * *

When you concentrate on negative things, you can waste a day when nothing brings you joy. But when you seek joy, it is everywhere!

—Debbie Boone

* * * * *

There is no more ineffective method of controlling human beings (of all ages) than the use of irritation and anger.

—James Dobson, *The Strong-Willed Child*

Laughter is an instant vacation.

—Milton Berle

✳ ✳ ✳ ✳ ✳

Luck is a matter of preparation meeting opportunity.

—Oprah Winfrey

✳ ✳ ✳ ✳ ✳

A ship in the harbor is perfectly safe, but that is not what a ship was created for.

—Author unknown

✳ ✳ ✳ ✳ ✳

A true measure of your worth includes all the benefits others have gained from your success.

—Cullen Hightower

✳ ✳ ✳ ✳ ✳

You miss 100 percent of the shots you never take.

—Wayne Gretzky

✳ ✳ ✳ ✳ ✳

It is difficult to steer a parked car, so get moving.

—Henrietta Mears

✳ ✳ ✳ ✳ ✳

I have missed more than 9,000 shots in my career. I have lost almost 300 games. On 26 occasions I have been entrusted to take the game-winning shot—and missed. And I have failed over and over and over again in my life. And *that* is why I succeed.

—Michael Jordan

Quotes

It's amazing what you can get done when you don't care who gets the credit.

—From a plaque on the office wall of former president Ronald Reagan

* * * * *

You never really understand a person until you consider things from his point of view.

—Harper Lee, *To Kill a Mocking Bird*

* * * * *

Life does not have to be perfect to be wonderful.

—Annette Funicello

* * * * *

There are two ways to live your life. One is as though nothing is a miracle. The other is as though everything is a miracle.

—Albert Einstein

* * * * *

It's pretty hard to tell what does bring happiness. Poverty and wealth have both failed.

—Ken Hubbard

Character

If you tell the truth, you don't have to remember anything.

—Mark Twain

* * * * *

Actions speak louder than words but not nearly as often.

—Mike Atkinson, Youth Specialties

* * * * *

Character is what you are in the dark.

—Dwight L. Moody

* * * * *

If men speak ill of you, live so that no one will believe them.

—Author unknown

* * * * *

Much may be known of a man's character by what excites his laughter.

—Goethe

* * * * *

Youth and beauty fade; character endures forever.

—Author unknown

Children and Family

If you don't take care of your children, I will.

—Shock rocker Marilyn Manson

* * * * *

People who do not like children are idiots, stupid and blockheads—because they have rejected the gift of God.

—Martin Luther

* * * * *

The difference I see between kids who make it and kids who don't, most often is one caring adult.

—Barbara Stagers, Young Life

* * * * *

A hundred years from now it will not matter what my bank account was, the sort of house I lived in or the kind of car I drove, but the world may be different because I was important in the life of a child.

—Author unknown

* * * * *

We put career, money and pleasure all ahead of family. The irony is, if we put family first, the rest tend to follow a lot more readily.

—Harvey Mackay

Evangelism

If you reach the family, you'll reach the world!

—Bill Bright

* * * * *

Nothing can move the gospel of Jesus Christ forward more effectively or thoroughly than healthy families.

—Blake Benge

* * * * *

Unless there is an element of risk in our exploits for God, there is no need for faith.

—Hudson Taylor

* * * * *

Don't tell me I have a friend in Jesus, until I have a friend in you.

—Ken Medema

* * * * *

When asked, "What motivated you to commit your life to the sick and dying?" Mother Teresa replied, "I haven't. I've committed my life to Jesus Christ and it just so happens I see Jesus on the faces of the sick and dying."

—Source unknown

Quotes

In my judgement the Christian life does not lead itself to much preaching or talking. It is best propagated by living it and applying it. When will you Christians really crown Jesus Christ as the Prince of Peace and proclaim Him through your deeds as the champion of the poor and oppressed?

—Mahatma Gandhi

✳ ✳ ✳ ✳ ✳

Preach the gospel at all times. If necessary, use words.

—St. Francis of Assisi

Evangelism

God

I have found there are three stages in every great work of God.

- First it is impossible.
- Then it is difficult.
- Then it is done.

—Hudson Taylor

* * * * *

Every limitation I have is an invitation by God to do for me what I cannot do for myself.

—Stephen F. Arterburn

* * * * *

First you ruthlessly remove hurry. Now you are ready to hear God.

—Author unknown

* * * * *

God does not call us to be successful, only to be faithful.

—Author unknown

* * * * *

There's only one catch. Like any other gift, the gift of grace can be ours only if we will reach out and take it. That is what faith is all about. But maybe being able to reach out and take it is a gift of grace too.

—Frederick Buechner

Kindness

One kind word can warm three winter months.

—Japanese Proverb

* * * * *

If someone were to pay you ten cents for every kind word you ever spoke and collect five cents for every unkind word, would you be rich or poor?

—Author unknown

* * * * *

Don't forget, a person's greatest emotional need is to feel appreciated.

—Author unknown

* * * * *

The greatest gift you can give another is the purity of your attention.

—Richard Moss, M.D.

Love

Love cures people—both the ones who give it and the ones who receive it.

—Karl Menninger

* * * * *

He loves not Christ at all who does not love Christ above all.

—Lance Zavitz

* * * * *

Before Christ, a man loves things and uses people. After Christ, he loves people and uses things

—Horace Wood

* * * * *

Love never asks how much must I do, but how much can I do.

—Frederick A. Agar, *Royal Service*

* * * * *

God is the source of love.
Christ is the proof of love.
Service is the expression of love.
Boldness is the outcome of love.

—Author unknown

* * * * *

Quotes

To love the whole world
For me is not a chore;
My only problem's
My neighbor next door.

—C. W. Vanderbergh

Funny but True

Karate is a form of martial arts in which people who have had years and years of training can, using only their hands and feet, make some of the worst movies known to the history of the world.

—Dave Barry

* * * * *

What is a committee? A group of unwilling picked from the unfit to do the necessary.

—Richard Harkness, *The New York Times*

* * * * *

For three days after death, hair and fingernails continue to grow but phone calls taper off.

—Johnny Carson

Contributors

Mike DeVries
Vice President, Family-Based Youth Ministry,
    YouthBuilders
San Juan Capistrano, California
16-year youth ministry veteran

Jim Liebelt
Director, YouthBuilders New England
Hull, Massachusetts
19-year youth ministry veteran

John Murphy
Associate Pastor for Youth Ministries, Steel Lake
    Presbyterian Church
Federal Way, Washington
18-year youth ministry veteran

Jean Tippit
Speaker, writer and youth ministry volunteer
Mobile, Alabama
17-year youth ministry veteran

Eric Wakeling
Junior High Pastor, Calvary Church
Santa Ana, California
8-year youth ministry veteran

Scripture Index

Old Testament

Genesis
1:1-38   61

Exodus
15:2   27
17:8-16   105

Leviticus
19:15   **81**
19:16   29
25:18   120

Numbers
12:10-16   100

Deuteronomy
11:18-23   41
15:7-11   16

Joshua
1:9   39

Ruth
1:16-18   105

1 Samuel
15:22   118
16:7   81, **109, 116**

1 Chronicles
28:20   39

Psalms
1:2-3   **41**
15   36
15:2-4   29
28:8   55
37:23-24   32
40:1-3   80
41:10   18
62:5-6   **90**
72:12-14   97
86:5   45
91:1-6   80
119:9,57-60   41
119:11,105   25
136   61, 125

Proverbs
2   31
3:5   74
3:5-6   31, **92, 120**
7   78
8:35-36   97
10:12   **63**
10:19   29
11:13   29
11:24-25   50
12:17   36
12:18   84
12:22   **36**
13:12   90
14:12   78
15:4   29
16:13   36
16:23-24   84
16:28   **29**
17:17   105
18:21   29
20:30   116
22:9   **50**
27:10   105
29:15   63
29:25   120
31:30   109, 116

Ecclesiastes
4:9-12   **105**
12:13-14   31

Isaiah
5:22   33
40:31   90
49:8-11   47
51:12   80
53:1-3   116
53:2   109
53:4-11   57
58:6-8,10   51

Jeremiah
17:7   120
31:3   42
31:34   45

Bold references indicate Key Verses.

Micah

6:8   80

Nahum

1:7   120

Zechariah

9:11-12   47

New Testament

Matthew

1:22-23	118
5:43-44	63
5:43-48	96
6:1-4	14, 76
6:33	**14**
7:13-14	**18**
10:8	**20**
10:16-18	106
11:25	121
12:34-36	84
12:35-37	29
13:1-23	94
13:44-46	122
15:18	84
17:19-21	74
17:20	39
18:21-35	96
18:3-4	33
24:45-51	94
25:23	71
25:31-46	16
25:34-45	51
26:13	71
28:18-20	106

Mark

4:23	118
8:35	103
11:23-24	100

Luke

6:38	50
9:23-24	**66**
9:23-27	71
9:26	103
9:61-62	49, 69
9:62	**12**
11:5-13	42
11:28	120

12:22-34	97
13:22-38	18
17:5-6	33
18:40-42	74
21:1-4	**112**

John

1:12	53
1:12-13	**45**
3:16-21	23
5:24	158
8:31-32	47, 82
8:31-36	25
10:7-11	97
12:42-46	14
13:14-15,34	20
14:3	90
14:15	94
14:23-24	16
15:7	92
15:7-14	25
15:12	20
15:12-17	105
15:18-25	106
17:3	122
20:24-28	116
20:29	74

Acts

5:1-11	76
9:36-43	100
11:23	86
12:5-19	92
15:32	86
20:35	50, **51**, 112

Romans

1:12	86
1:16-17	71
1:19	61

Bold references indicate Key Verses.

1:20	61	**Galatians**	
2:1-2	121	**1:10**	14, **76**
5:1-5	90	2:20	66
5:10	57	3:1-5,26-29	53
6:15-23	47	3:26—4:7	45
6:23	18, **33**	5:13	20
8:12-17	45	6:10	50
8:17	**53**, 122	6:15	23
8:28	120	6:17	116
8:31-39	42, 125		
10:15	109	**Ephesians**	
12:1	71	1:7	57
12:1-2	18	1:3,7-8,13-14,18-19	53
12:9	76	1:14	122
12:9-10	81	2:13	57
12:9-19	31	3:13	116
12:20	51	3:16-19	42, 125
13:13-14	33	**4:1**	**59**
14:12	101	4:2-3	59
15:2	86	4:11-16	94
15:4	90	4:22-24	23
		4:29	84, 86
1 Corinthians		**4:31-32**	**96**
1:17-18	57	**5:15-16**	**101**
1:18	**118**	6:7	20
1:22-25	118		
1:27	27, **121**	**Philippians**	
2:3-5	55	1:6	12
2:6-16	82	**1:21**	66, **71**, **106**
4:2	101	1:27-28	103
6:18	78	2:5-11	118
9:24-25	**31**	**3:7-8**	**122**
9:24-27	49	3:12-13,15-16	69
		3:12-16	31
2 Corinthians		3:13-14	49
1:3-4	**80**	**3:14**	**69**
2:15	103		
4:8-9	**32**	**Colossians**	
5:17	**23**	**1:19-22**	**57**
6:3-7	36	2:13-14	53
6:10	112	4:5	101
8:1-15	112		
9:5-7	50	**1 Thessalonians**	
9:6-15	112	1:3,5	90
9:12-14	51	2:7-8	63
12:9	**27**	3:2	86
12:9-10	**55**	4:17	90
13:4	55	**5:11**	63, **86**

Bold references indicate Key Verses.

1 Timothy

1:6-7	69
2:1-3	100
2:1-5	92
4:12	59, 74
5:13	29
6:18-19	112

2 Timothy

2:10-13	32, 49
2:11-13	66
3:16-17	**25**, 41
4:1-5	118
4:2	86
4:7	12, **49**

Titus

3:1-3	96
3:3-8	23

Hebrews

3:13	78, 86
4:11-13	25
10:25	86
11:1	**74**
11:25-26	**78**
11:32-34	27
12:1-2	31, **97**
12:1-13	71
12:2-3	118
12:3-4	116

James

1:2-4	39
1:2-5	112
1:12	**39**
2:1-9	81
2:1-13	121
3:1-12	29
3:3-8,11-12	84
3:9-10	**84**
3:13	59
5:13-15	**100**
5:13-18	92

1 Peter

1:4	122
2:20-22	106
3:3-4	81
3:3-5	109

3:4-5	116
3:10	78
4:1-6	59
4:3-5	33
5:6-11	92

2 Peter

3:17-18	**94**

1 John

1:7-8,10	47
1:9	**47**
2:7-17	25
2:15-17	18
2:17	59
3:1	**42**
3:16-23	16, 42
3:18	**16**
4:1	**82**
4:2-6	82
4:7-8	125
4:10	**125**
5:2-13	14
5:4-5	32, 49

Revelation

1:5	57
2:10	**103**

Bold references indicate Key Verses.

Topical Index

A

appearances   18, 76, 81, 109, 116, 121
attitude   32

B

blessings   20, 112

C

challenges   39
Christmas   118
comfort   80
commitment   66
Cross   57

D

difficulty   55

E

enjoying Christ   53

F

fears and doubts   69
fellowship   105
following God   94
following others   18
forgiveness   45, 47, 96

G

God's love   42, 45, 125
God's promises   125
God's revelation   61

H

helping others   16, 50, 51, 112, 121
holy living   59
honesty/integrity   36, 47, 76, 109
hope   90

K

kindness   20, 16

L

listening to God   94
love of a child   33, 63
loving your neighbor   51, 81

M

miracles   33, 57, 106
motivation   14

N

need for God   55

P

peer pressure   103
persistence   12, 32, 42, 49, 94
power of God   23, 25, 71, 97
power of words   29, 63, 84, 86
prayer   92, 100

R

relying on God   74
response to Christ's love   20, 66, 125

S

sacrifice   116
salvation   45, 53, 97, 118, 122
sharing   51
sin   78
standing up for Christ   66, 71, 103, 106
success   31

T

testing what you hear   82
time   59, 101
time with God   20, 41, 61
trust   74, 120

U

unexpected blessings   39, 55

W

weaknesses   27

www.youthbuilders.com

Reach & Impact Young People, Strengthen Families and Youth Workers, and Change Lives Forever!

Training

YouthBuilders offers a full range of training events from one-day seminars to weeklong conferences designed to equip youth workers, parents, and students. For a complete listing of events, contact training@youthbuilders.com or visit www.youthbuilders.com.

YouthBuilders.com

A family-based youth ministry web destination where youth workers and parents can learn the latest in training methods for guiding and influencing today's youth; sign up for our FREE monthly Fresh Ideas Youth Worker newsletters and our Good Advice Parent newsletters that are full of practical information, encouragement and valuable insights; and check out the huge selection of proven resources. Youth workers and parents can easily print out the latest guidelines for helping young people navigate the challenges faced when growing up in today's world.

Resources

YouthBuilders has an incredible selection of helpful resources for youth workers, parents and students including training videos, devotionals, curriculum and books. Visit our web site for a complete description.

YouthBuilders Radio

Jim Burns' drama/commentaries are on stations across the United States and Canada. Through drama, music, commentaries, and humor, Jim's radio program provides guidance and counsel on the most current issues facing today's family. To find a local station visit www.youthbuilders.com.

www.youthbuilders.com • 1-800-397-9725

32236 Paseo Adelanto, Suite D, San Juan Capistrano, California 92675

More Great Ways to Reach and Teach Young People

So You Want to Be a Wise Guy
An outrageous group study for junior high
Manual
ISBN 08307.29178

Dave's Complete Guide to Junior High Ministry
An all-in-one, practical, hands-on guide for everything relating to junior high ministry
Dave Veerman
Paperback
ISBN 08307.27604

GP4U (God's Plan for You)
A middle school/junior high group study
Kara Eckmann Powell
Reproducible
ISBN 08307.24060

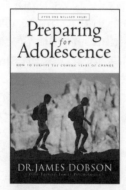

Preparing for Adolescence
Dr. James Dobson
Paperback
ISBN 08307.24974

Guide to Childhood Development
Mass
ISBN 08307.24990

Family Guide and Workbook
Manual
ISBN 08307.25016

Growth Guide Manual
ISBN 08307.25024

Group Guide
ISBN 08307.25008

Family Tape Pack—8 Audiocassettes
ISBN 08307.26357

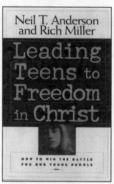

Leading Teens to Freedom in Christ
How to win the battle for our young people
Neil T. Anderson
and *Rich Miller*
Paperback
ISBN 08307.18400

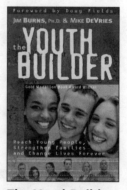

The YouthBuilder
Reaching young people for Christ and changing lives forever
Jim Burns
and *Mike DeVries*
Paperback
ISBN 08307.29232

Gospel Light

Available at your local Christian bookstore
www.gospellight.com

043021

Pulse
GOD'S WORD FOR A JR. HIGH WORLD

> "This is the best junior high/middle school curriculum to come out in years. Creativity and Biblical integrity are evident on every page. Students will love it."
> —Jim Burns, Ph.D.
> President
> National Institute of Youth Ministry

Young people between the ages of 11 and 14 are the most open to who Jesus is and what a life with Him offers. Reach them with Pulse—designed especially for them!

Throughout the cutting-edge series, three categories of study help junior highers understand and apply God's Word in their lives: Biblical, Life Issues and Discipleship.

Connect with junior highers—get all the Pulse studies!

#1 Christianity: the Basics
ISBN 08307.24079

#2 Prayer
ISBN 08307.24087

#3 Friends
ISBN 08307.24192

#4 Teachings of Jesus
ISBN 08307.24095

#5 Followers of Christ
ISBN 08307.24117

#6 Teens of the Bible
ISBN 08307. 24125

#7 Life at School
ISBN 08307.25083

#8 Miracles of Jesus
ISBN 08307.25091

#9 Home and Family
ISBN 08307.25105

#10 Genesis
ISBN 08307.25113

#11 Fruit of the Spirit
ISBN 08307.25474

#12 Feelings & Emotions
ISBN 08307.25482

#13 Peer Pressure
ISBN 08307.25490

#14 Reaching Your World
ISBN 08307.25504

Available at your local Christian bookstore.
www.gospellight.com

Gospel Light

041633

More from Jim Burns, the Youth Ministry Expert!

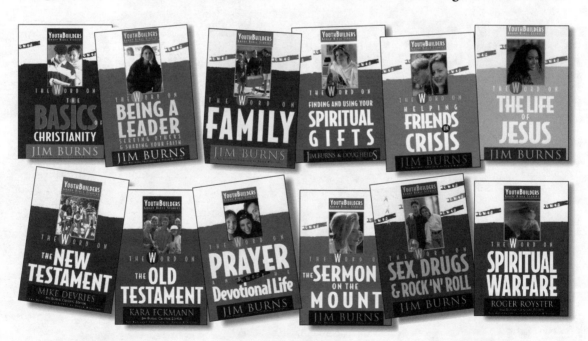

Wake 'Em Up!

This fresh-roasted blend of sizzling hot resources helps you turn youth meetings into dynamic events that kids look forward to. Successfully field-tested in youth groups and edited by youth expert **Jim Burns, Fresh Ideas** will wake 'em up and get your group talking.

Bible Study Outlines and Messages
ISBN 08307.18850

Case Studies, Talk Sheets and Starters
ISBN 08307.18842

Games, Crowdbreakers & Community Builders
ISBN 08307.18818

Illustrations, Stories and Quotes to Hang Your Message On
ISBN 08307.18834

Incredible Retreats
ISBN 08307.24036

Missions and Service Projects
ISBN 08307.18796

Skits and Dramas
ISBN 08307.18826

Worship Experiences
ISBN 08307.24044

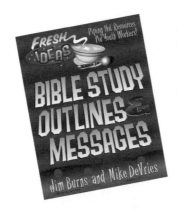

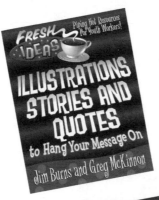

Gospel Light

To wake up your youth, contact your local Christian bookstore. **www.gospellight.com**